Relational Database Design for Starters:
Explained through a Case Study in Microsoft Access

Akmal Masood

International Standard Book Number: 978-1-4357-0798-6

For Sales, please contact

orders@lulu.com

To my friend, Les Prescott, for his friendship.

Table of Contents

Chapter 1

Introduction

A database is a collection of data that is organized so that it can easily be accessed, managed and updated. A database can be as simple as a single list of phone numbers or as complex as a bank account. These days the term is used for computerized systems that can store data in such a way that a computer program can easily retrieve and manipulate the data. Consider you go to your family doctor's office for an appointment. The secretary asks your first name and last name. Then she goes to the back and looks for your file. She looks for a file with your last name. She can find your file easily as the clinic may be taking a limited number of patients. Consider the clinic has one million patients, and then her job to find a file would become more difficult. What about finding all the patients with insomnia? It would be nearly impossible to go through one million patient's records and look for people with insomnia. This is a good example of a non-computerized database. A computer will do the same job with in seconds.

You may wonder what is the difference between a database and Database Management System? A database is a collection of data. In order to keep the data in your database under control, you need software known as **DBMS** (DataBase Management System).

There are different ways in which data can be modeled. Hierarchical, Network and Relational are three such models. The most widely used is the relational model. Dr Edgar Codd came up with the original idea of relational model. This book attempts to introduce the concepts and ideas behind the relational model. A DBMS in which the data is stored in the form of tables and the relationship among the data is also stored in the form of tables is called a **Relational** DBMS. To further simplify the matter, an RDBMS (Relational Database Management System) such as Microsoft Access will be used to build a database to show how easy it is to use a database to store data about customers, products, orders, employees etc.
The four core components of a database are

- Tables
- Forms
- Queries
- Reports

Tables

A table is the basic data container. All the data stored in a database is stored in tables. Think of a table as the container in which the data sits and the other three (Forms, Queries & Reports) as devices which manipulate the data contained in the table. Each table contains information about a specific topic. A table that contains information about customers might look like the one shown in Figure 1.1

Customer					
CustomerId	FirstName	LastName	Address	City	Phone
7	Nancy	Wong	87 Polk St	Kirkland	675-123-1234
8	Andrew	Jackson	7 Davinci Blvd	Portland	375-123-2345
9	Michael	King	83 Jefferson Blvd	Richmond	176-123-2456

Figure 1.1

Forms

A form is a convenient way to enter or find data in tables. You can enter data directly in a table but it is often easier to enter data in a form. This is especially true if the person entering the data in the database is unfamiliar with the software. Forms can be made more attractive and easy to use than tables. Forms are used for data entry, editing and deleting operations. A form showing information from Customer table is shown in figure 1.2.

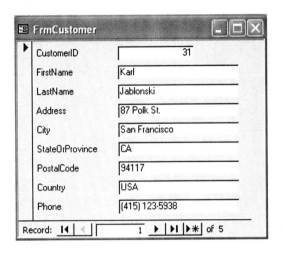

Figure 1.2

Queries

A query is a question that we ask of the database. A query retrieves specific data from a table or from two or more related tables. A query can retrieve data that meet specific criteria set by you. Queries are used within databases because the tables hold large amounts of data, and we want to deal with just a subset of that data. Consider you want to find all customers from California. You would create a query on Customer table and the criteria for the query would be StateOrProvice = CA. Figure 1.3 show the result of such a query.

QryCustomer

FirstName	LastName	Address	City	StateOrProvince	PostalCode	Phone
Karl	Jablonski	87 Polk St.	San Francisco	CA	94117	(415) 123-5938

Figure 1.3

Reports

A report is a printed output from a table or a query. Consider you want a list of all of your customers from Customer table sorted by first name. You would use a report to print out such a list from a printer as shown in figure 1.4

RptCustomer

FirstName	LastName	Address	City
Karl	Jablonski	87 Polk St.	San Francisco
Liu	Wong	722 Davinci Blvd	Kirkland
Liz	Nixon	89 Jefferson Way	Portland
Paula	Wilson	2817 Milton Dr.	Albuquerque
Yoshi	Latimer	89 Polk St.	Elgin

Figure 1.4

Single Table Database

Within a database, the data is stored in tables. A simple database will contain a single table, while more complex ones may contain many tables. For example, if you want to keep your address book about customers in a database, then a single table is perfect for this kind of use. Figure 1.5 shows an address book for customers.

Customer Address book

FirstName	LastName	Address	City	StateOrProvince	PostalCode	Phone
Karl	Jablonski	87 Polk St.	San Francisco	CA	94117	(415) 123-5938
Liu	Wong	722 Davinci Blvd	Kirkland	WA	98034	(206) 123-8257
Liz	Nixon	89 Jefferson Way	Portland	OR	97201	(503) 123-3612
Paula	Wilson	2817 Milton Dr.	Albuquerque	NM	87110	(505) 123-3620
Yoshi	Latimer	89 Polk St.	Elgin	OR	97827	(503) 555-6874

Figure 1.5

Suppose that all your customers in Figure 1.5 enroll in a school and become students. You are assigned the duty of keeping the list of student contact information and enrollment information. Each list of information pertains to a specific subject and student contact information. Figure 1.6 shows the table that you have created from both kind of information

Student

ClassTitle	ClassDescription	FirstName	LastName	Address	City	PostalCode	Phone
Hist 101	Medieval History	Karl	Jablonski	87 Polk St.	San Francisco	94117	(415) 123-5938
Hist 101	Medieval History	Liu	Wong	722 Davinci Blvd	Kirkland	98034	(206) 123-8257
Hist 101	Medieval History	Liz	Nixon	89 Jefferson Way	Portland	97201	(503) 123-3612
Hist 101	Medieval History	Paula	Wilson	2817 Milton Dr.	Albuquerque	87110	(505) 123-3620
Hist 101	Medieval History	Yoshi	Latimer	89 Polk St.	Elgin	97827	(503) 555-6874
Phy 201	Thermodynamics	Karl	Jablonski	87 Polk St.	San Francisco	94117	(415) 123-5938
Phy 201	Thermodynamics	Liu	Wong	722 Davinci Blvd	Kirkland	98034	(206) 123-8257
Phy 201	Thermodynamics	Liz	Nixon	89 Jefferson Way	Portland	97201	(503) 123-3612
Phy 201	Thermodynamics	Paula	Wilson	2817 Milton Dr.	Albuquerque	87110	(505) 123-3620
Phy 201	Thermodynamics	Yoshi	Latimer	89 Polk St.	Elgin	97827	(503) 555-6874
Chem 301	Organic Chemistry	Karl	Jablonski	87 Polk St.	San Francisco	94117	(415) 123-5938
Chem 301	Organic Chemistry	Liu	Wong	722 Davinci Blvd	Kirkland	98034	(206) 123-8257
Chem 301	Organic Chemistry	Liz	Nixon	89 Jefferson Way	Portland	97201	(503) 123-3612
Chem 301	Organic Chemistry	Paula	Wilson	2817 Milton Dr.	Albuquerque	87110	(505) 123-3620
Chem 301	Organic Chemistry	Yoshi	Latimer	89 Polk St.	Elgin	97827	(503) 555-6874

Figure 1.6

Now we have to explain why a single table or a flat file table is not the right choice for this situation.

Redundant Data

There is a considerable amount of repeated data in this table. There are 5 students enrolled in 3 subjects. This makes the number of required rows 15. Each time a student enrolls in a subject, you have to type all his or her information again instead of just the additional subject information. Let us say there are 100 students and each one enrolls in the minimum of 5 subjects. This makes your job harder needing 500 rows. This repeated information wastes a lot of disk space and potentially slows down the system.

Typographical Errors

Many people will be entering data into the table. Will they be consistent? People make typographical errors. Each time they enter data into a table; there is a chance of a spelling mistake in any of the records.

Updating Data

Suppose one of the student, Liz Nixon gets married and elects to adopt her husband's last name. To keep the data consistent, someone have to go through all data and manually change her name. You may change the data in most rows but in some you may miss the update. Now you have ended up with the same person showing two last names.

Multiple Tables Database

In a multiple table database (Relational database), each student's contact information and course information is recorded only once. Each student's record is assigned an identification (ID). Each course record is assigned an identification. Now to convert the table in figure 1.6 to relational tables, we have to create 3 tables. We call the table containing student information as Student. The table containing course information, we call Course. A third table containing the link between the two tables is called StudentCourse. All three tables are shown in figure 1.7.

Student

StudentID	FirstName	LastName	Address	City	PostalCode	Phone
1	Karl	Jablonski	87 Polk St.	San Francisco	94117	(415) 123-5938
2	Liu	Wong	722 Davinci Blvd	Kirkland	98034	(206) 123-8257
3	Liz	Nixon	89 Jefferson Way	Portland	97201	(503) 123-3612
4	Paula	Wilson	2817 Milton Dr.	Albuquerque	87110	(505) 123-3620
5	Yoshi	Latimer	89 Polk St.	Elgin	97827	(503) 555-6874

Course

CourseID	ClassTitle	ClassDescription
1	Hist 101	Medieval History
2	Phy 201	Thermodynamics
3	Chem 301	Oragnic Chemistry

StudentCourse

StudentID	CourseID
1	1
1	2
1	3
2	1
2	2
2	3
3	1
3	2
3	3
4	1
4	2
4	3
5	1
5	2
5	3

Figure 1.7

As you can see in figure 1.7, the link table StudentCourse contains the information specifying who is having what course. As an example, the first 3 rows in StudentCourse table shows that the student with ID # 1 (Karl) is enrolled in Courses with IDs 1, 2 & 3 which are History 101, Physics 201 & Chemistry 301.

A database that contains two or more linked tables is called a **Relational Database**. Now let us see how multiple tables can remove the last three problems that were discussed in the previous section.

Redundant Data

You have to ask your self a question. How many times student information (FirstName, LastName, Address, etc) was repeated? How many times course information (ClassTitle and ClassDescription) was repeated? In figure 1.7, the answer to both questions is only once. In figure 1.6, each student's information (look at FirstName column) was repeated 3 times and each course's information (look at ClassTitle column) was repeated 5 times. We can conclude that by using multiple tables we can save lots of disk space which eventually can make the system run faster.

Typographical Errors

You have seen in figure 1.7 that each record is typed once. There is less chance of a typing error if you type a record once. In case you make a typing mistake, it is easy to locate the record and correct the mistake.

Updating Data

Now if Liz Nixon gets married and elects to adopt her husband's last name, it wouldn't be a big problem to change her last name in the database as the data has to be changed only once in the Student table.

You should be convinced by now that multiple tables are the only way in which to store complex data efficiently. The next chapter explains the basic definitions and concepts behind relational databases.

Chapter 2

The Entity-Relationship Model

Charles Bachman formalized schema diagrams in 1960. Schema diagram is a diagrammatic representation of the organization of a database. He used rectangles to denote record types and arrows from one record to another to show relationships. In 1976 Peter Chen proposed the Entity-Relationship (ER) model as a way to unify and depict relationship views. Simply stated the ER model is a conceptual data model that views the real world as entities and relationships. A basic component of the model is the Entity-Relationship diagram which is used to visually represent data objects. Figure 2.1 shows some of the notations used in Chen's ER modeling. For the database designer, the utility of the ER model is:

- It maps well to the relational model. The constructs used in the ER model can easily be transformed into relational tables.

- It is simple and easy to understand with a minimum of training. The model can be used by the database designer to communicate the design to the end user that is independent of the software.

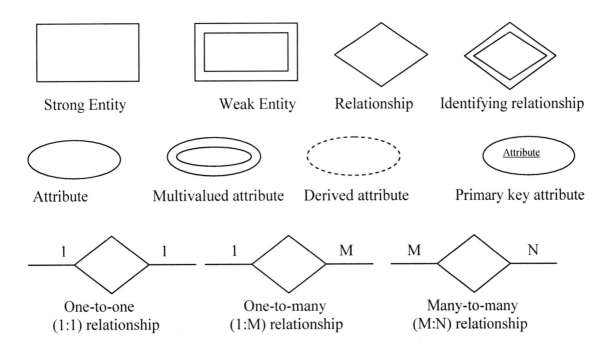

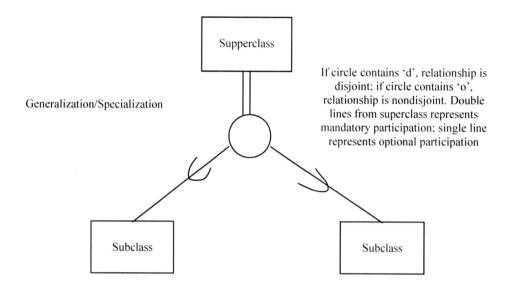

Generalization/Specialization

If circle contains 'd', relationship is disjoint; if circle contains 'o', relationship is nondisjoint. Double lines from superclass represents mandatory participation; single line represents optional participation

Figure 2.1 Chen notations for ER modeling

ER Notation

There is no standard for representing data objects in ER diagrams. Each modeling methodology uses its own notation. The original notations used by Chen as shown in figure 2.1 are widely used in academics texts and journals but rarely seen in either CASE (computer assisted systems engineering) tools or publications by non-academics. Today, there are a number of notations used. Among the more common are Crow's foot and IDEFIX. Figure 2.2 shows Crow's Foot notations. This is a popular model supported by many CASE tools. Notations from Chen's model and Crow's Foot model will be used in this book.

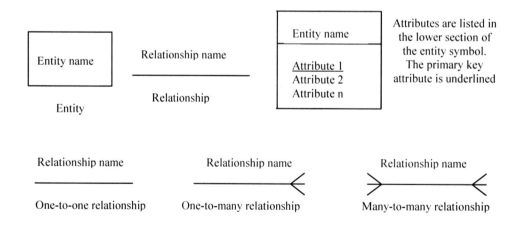

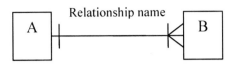

One-to-many relationship with
mandatory participation from both
entities A and B

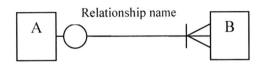

One-to-many relationship with optional
participation for entity A and mandatory
participation for entity B

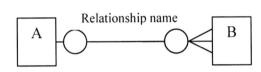

One-to-many relationship with optional
participation for both entities A and B

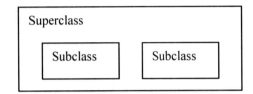

'Box-in-box' convention is used to
represent generalization/specialization

Figure 2.2 Crow's Foot notation for ER modeling

Components of ER model
The following are the key components of ER model
- Entity
- Attributes
- Relationships
- Cardinality
- Degree of relationship

Entity
An entity is any type of object that we wish to store data about. An object can have
physical existence or a conceptual existence. Some examples of these types of entities are
Person: Employee, Student, Patient
Place: State, Region, Country
Object: Machine, Building, Automobile
Event: Sale, Registration, Renewal
Concept: Account, Course, Work Center

The entity name is generally written in Singular. Employee rather than Employees.
Vendor rather than Vendors. Figure 2.3 shows an Employee entity and its equivalent
relational table.

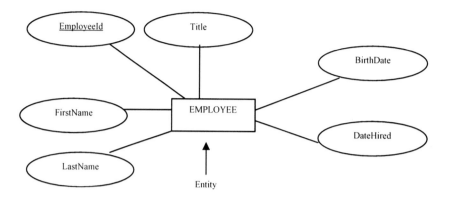

Employee

EmployeeId	FirstName	LastName	Title	BirthDate	DateHired
7	Nancy	Wong	SalesRep	8/11/1971	1/2/2000
8	Andrew	Jackson	SalesRep	3/5/1973	5/1/1999
9	Michael	King	SalesRep	4/15/1967	5/1/1999

Figure 2.3 Showing an Employee entity and its equivalent relational table

In a relational model, each entity in ER diagram becomes a relational table. Each table consists of rows (horizontal) and columns (vertical). Each row contains the data about one employee, and the data contained in one row is known as a record. Row refers explicitly to the table and record refers to the data that is contained in a row. The term column and field are interchangeable. Column explicitly refers to the table and field refers more to the data that is contained in a column.

Entity instance

A single occurrence of an Entity type is called *entity instance*. For example Employee is an entity type where Nancy Wong, Andrew Jackson & Michael King are its entity instances. Each row in the relational table is known as an entity instance in the ER model.

Strong entity

An entity that exists independently of other entity types is called a Strong entity. For example Employee, Customer etc are examples of a strong entity.

Weak entity

An entity whose existence depends on some other entity is called a Weak entity. In the above example if an Employee has dependents then Employee is a strong entity where Dependent is a weak entity as the Dependent entity depends on the existence of Employee entity.

Attributes

The data that we want to keep about each entity is called its attributes. For Employee entity the attributes can be EmployeeID, Name, Address, PhoneNumber, EmploymentDate and any other information that we want to keep about Employee entity. Each attribute in ER model becomes a column in a relational table. Figure 2.4 shows an entity with its different attributes.

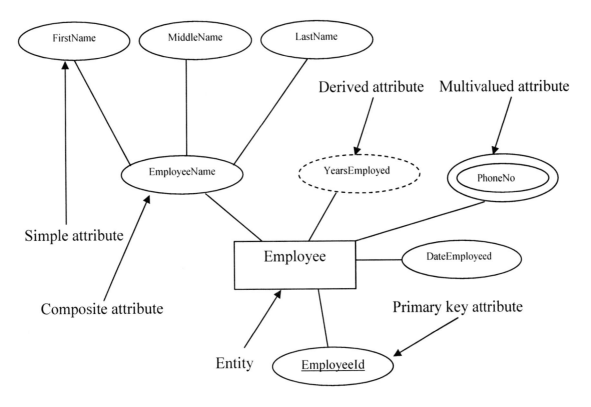

Figure 2.4 An ER diagram showing an entity with its different attributes

Simple or Atomic attribute

A simple attribute cannot be broken down into smaller components eg an EmployeeID in Employee entity shown in figure 2.4.

Composite Attributes

Some attributes can be broken down into meaningful component parts. In the Employee entity, EmployeeName is an example of composite attribute. An EmployeeName is composed of first name, middle name and last name.

Single valued attribute

A Single valued attribute is an attribute that can take one value for a given entity instance. For example, an employee in Employee entity has a single value for the EmployeeID.

Multivalued attribute

A Multivalued attribute is an attribute that can take more than one value for a given entity instance. For example, an employee in Employee entity has more than one PhoneNumber.

Derived attribute

A Derived attribute is an attribute whose values can be calculated from related attribute values. For example finding out how long an employee has been with the company. You could calculate the length of time from DateEmployeed attribute and current date.

Primary key or unique identifier attribute

If an attribute can be thought of as a unique identifier for an entity, it is called a *candidate key*. When a candidate key is chosen to be the unique identifier, it becomes the *primary key* for the entity. Attributes that are unique identifiers are usually underlined. A unique identifier can be an attribute or a combination of attributes. For the Employee entity, EmployeeId is its primary key.

Foreign Key

A Primary key is called a Foreign key when it is referred to from another table. In figure 2.5, the Primary key EmployeeId (from Employee entity) is a foreign key in Order entity. We will discuss this further in topics ahead.

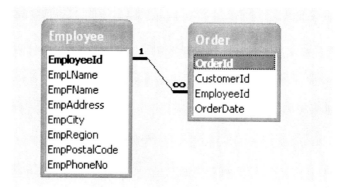

Figure 2.5

Relationship

Relationship is a meaningful association among entities. Usually a verb or preposition that connects two entities implies a relationship.

Relationship type

Relationship type is a named association between entity types. For example a Customer (entity) *places* (relationship) an Order (entity), a Student (entity) *enrolls* (relationship) in a Course (entity).

Entity instances are related because an action was taken, thus it is appropriate to choose a verb phrase for the label. This verb phrase should be in the present tense and descriptive. There are many ways to represent a relationship. One way is by placing a single verb phrase in a diamond to represent a relationship. Another way of representing a relationship is just by a line without the diamond, but with two relationship names, one for each direction of the relationship. Both notations have the same meaning, so you can use either format. Figure 2.6 shows both notations.

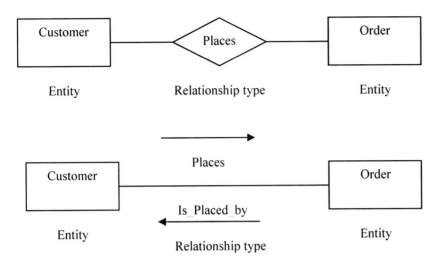

Figure 2.6 An ER diagram showing relationship

Relationship instance

Relationship instance is an association between entity instances. Consider a Customer Places an Order relationship. Customer is an entity, it will have many customers (Cindy, Alex, ..). Order is another entity it will have many orders (Order #1, 2, 3 ..) . A customer can place one or many orders. A customer Cindy places an order #1 for a notebook computer. She places another order # 2 for a printer. There are two relationships, one between Cindy and Order # 1 and the other is between Cindy and Order # 2. Each one of this relationship is a *relationship instance*. Strictly speaking 'Places' is a *relationship type* consisting of a number of *relationships* between entity types. Most of the times the distinction between relationship and relationship type is dropped and both are given the name relationship.

Identifying relationship

Identifying relationship is the relationship between a weak entity type and its owner. In our example in figure 2.7, the "Has" relationship between Employee (strong entity) and Dependent (weak entity) is an identifying relationship.

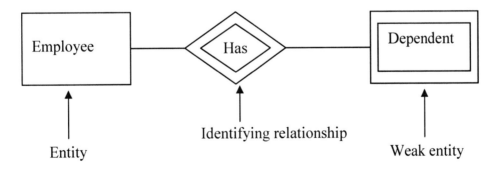

Figure 2.7 Identifying relationship

12

Cardinality

Cardinality is the constraint on the number of instances of one entity that can participate in a relationship with each instance of another entity. Cardinality depends on business rules. **Business rule** is a statement that defines or constrains some aspect of the business. Consider the example of a customer having a bank account. Generally one account is assigned to one customer. If a business allows an account being shared by many customers, then there is nothing stopping them. Therefore, when you think of cardinality, think of the business rules applying to the relationship.

One-to-one, 1:1, means that each entity can only participate once.

One-to-many, 1:M, means that one entity can participate once, the other can participate many times.

Many-to-many, M:N, means that every entity can participate many times.

There are two directions of a relationship type. Each is named and each has a minimum degree and a maximum degree. There are three symbols used to show the degree of relationship. A circle means zero, a line (upright) means one and a Crow's foot means many. To depict minimum and maximum cardinalities, the cardinality symbols are placed adjacent to each entity type in a relationship. The minimum cardinality symbol appears towards the relationship name while the maximum cardinality symbol appears toward the entity type as shown in Figure 2.8.

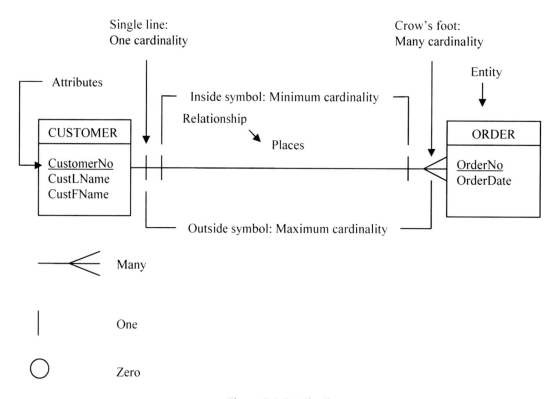

Figure 2.8 Cardinality

A minimum cardinality of one or more indicates a mandatory relationship. In our example in figure 2.8, from the Customer side (left to right), participation in the Places relationship is mandatory for each Customer entity due to the minimum cardinality one. From the order side (right to left) the participation in the places relationship is also mandatory for each Order entity as the minimum cardinality is one. A mandatory relationship makes the entity type existence dependent on the relationship

A minimum cardinality of 0 indicates an optional relationship. Let us assume that you created a database for your business cards and want to track Name and Address. Consider the relationship between Name entity and Address entity in figure 2.9. From the Name side (left to right), a Name can be associated with 0 address (person is not having a work address as he is not working) or exactly one address (person works at one location). From the Address side (right to left), one address can be associated with 0, 1 or many names (many people may be working at the same address). Figure 2.9 show the optional relationship

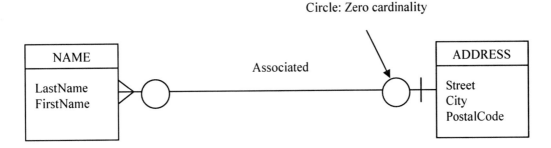

Figure 2.9 Optional relationship

Reading Entity Relationship Diagrams

You read the diagrams from left to right and then from right to left. Figure 2.10 shows reading an entity relationship diagram. In our case of Customer-Order relationship in Figure 2.10, you read the relationships as follows.

From left to right, a Customer can place a minimum of one order or a maximum of many orders.
From right to left, an order can be placed by a minimum of one customer and a maximum of one customer (For a maximum, we do not allow the same order assigned to more than one customer, therefore, the maximum is one order). This is a mandatory one relationship.

Let us see the same relationship from another angle and put it in to two questions. Both questions must begin with the word 'one'.

From left to right (From Customer to Order):
Question: One customer places how many orders?
Answer: The minimum is one and the maximum is many
Place 1 for minimum and crowfoot (many) for maximum next to Order entity

From right to left (From Order to Customer):
Question: One order is placed by how many customers?
Answer: The minimum is one and the maximum is one. (Business rule: We do not want the same order to be assigned to more than one customer)
Place 1 for minimum and 1 for maximum next to Customer entity as shown in figure 2.10

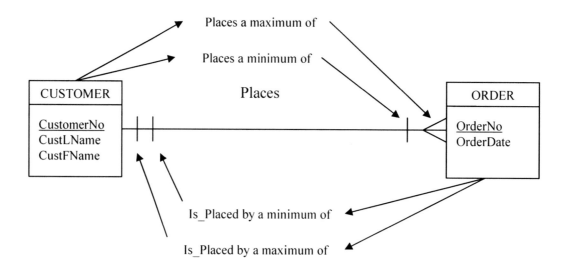

Figure 2.10 Reading an entity relationship diagram

Degree of a relationship
In terms of connectivity, a relationship can include one or more entities. The degree of a relationship is the number of entities that participate in the relationship. The three most common relationships in ER models are Unary, binary and ternary. Relationship of degree 1 is called Unary, relationship of degree 2 is binary which is the most common and relationship of degree 3 is Ternary.

Unary relationship
A relationship between the instances of a Single entity type is called a Unary relationship. Unary relationships are also called recursive relationships. A Person (single instance of an entity) Marries a Person (Single instance of an entity). Business rule: Here we assume that polygamy is not legal. An Employee (single instance of an entity) Supervise other Employee (many instances of an entity). Figure 2.11 shows two different examples of unary relationship.

15

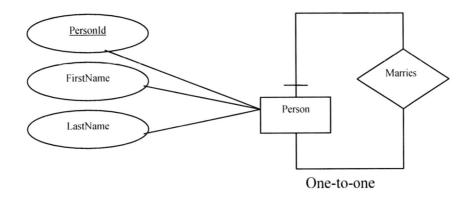

One-to-one

Figure 2.11 (a) Unary relationship

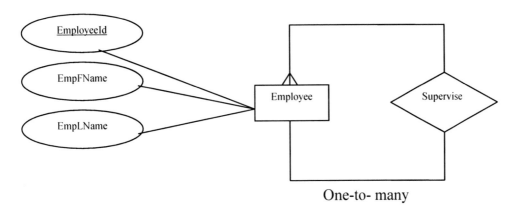

One-to- many

Figure 2.11 (b) Unary relationship

During the definition of Entity we said that in a relational model each entity is shown as a table. To implement the one-to-one relationship shown in figure 2.11 (a), a foreign key attribute (Spouse) is added to the Person table that references the primary key PersonId as shown in figure 2.12. This foreign key is called **recursive foreign key**. Here we assume that nobody has taken other person's last name after marriage. Looking at the Spouse column of this table we could say that Andrew Jackson (PersonId = 1) is married to Nancy Wong (PersonId = 3) and Rob Anderson (PersonId = 2) is married to Julia Lee (PersonId = 4).

Person

PersonId	FirstName	LastName	Spouse
1	Andrew	Jackson	3
2	Rob	Anderson	4
3	Nancy	Wong	1
4	Julia	Lee	2

Figure 2.12 Implementing one-to-one unary relationship

The one-to-many unary relationship in figure 2.11(b) can be implemented as a single table as shown in figure 2.13. Here again we add a foreign key (Supervisor) to the Employee table that references the primary key (EmployeeId). Looking at the Supervisor column of the Employee table, we could say Tom Lam (EmployeeId = 5) is the supervisor of all the employees in Employee table. Tom Lam himself doesn't have a supervisor.

Employee

EmployeeId	EmpFName	EmpLName	Supervisor
1	Andrew	Jackson	5
2	Rob	Anderson	5
3	Nancy	Wong	5
4	Julia	Lee	5
5	Tom	Lam	

Figure 2.13 Implementing one-to-many unary relationship

The third kind of unary relationship is many-to-many. Consider the example of taking a Course. A Course may require zero or many courses before starting a Course. On the other hand the same Course may be a part of zero or many Courses. This is a many-to-many unary relationship. Figure 2.14 shows this scenario.

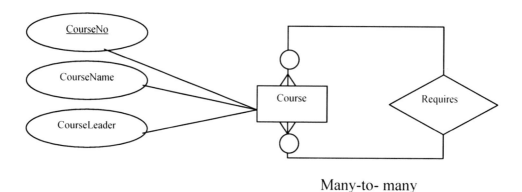

Many-to- many

Figure 2.14 Many-to-many unary relationship

Generally an entity is shown by a single table as we have done in the previous examples. In case of Many-to-many unary relationship two tables are needed. One is to represent the entity and another to represent the many-to-many associative relationship with itself.

Course

CourseNo	CourseName	CourseLeader
1	Chemistry	Mr. Black
2	Adv Chemistry	Mr. Parson
3	Physics	Mr. Lee
4	Adv Physics	Mr. Hung

Requirement

CourseNo	RequirementNo	EntryTest
1		No
2	1	Yes
3		No
4	3	Yes

Figure 2.15 Tables representing a unary many-to-many relationship

For Course table, we create another table called Requirement. The primary key for Requirement table is a composite key consisting of CourseNo and RequirementNo. Both these attributes takes their values from the primary key for Course table which is CourseNo. EntryTest is a non key attribute of the relationship Requires. Figure 2.15 shows the final tables after converting the many-to-many unary relationship to tables. By looking at the Requirement table, you would notice that CourseNo 1 and 3 do not have any requirement. On the other hand CourseNo 2 requires course 1 and CourseNo 4 requires Course 3. For any further discussion on associative relationship, please refer to the topic of Associative entity.

Binary relationship

A relationship between the instances of two entity types is called Binary relationship. This is the most common type of relationship. There are three types of binary relationships and they are One-to-one, One-to-many and Many-to-many.

Figure 2.16 shows a One-to-one binary relationship. This is an example of an employee managing a store relationship. To find the cardinality between the two entities you ask the following questions

Question: One Employee Manages how many Stores?

Answer: The minimum is 0 and the maximum is 1.

Place 0 and 1 next to Store entity.

Question: One Store is Managed by how many employees?

Answer: The minimum 1 and the maximum 1.

Place both 1's next to Employee entity.

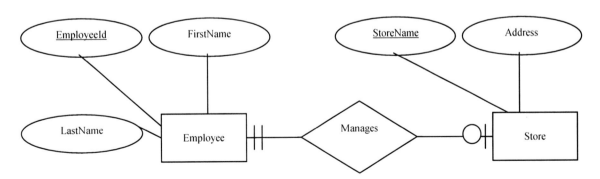

Figure 2.16 One-to-one binary relationship

The association from the Employee to Store is an optional one since any Employee may or may not manage a Store. The association from Store to Employee is a mandatory one since each store must be managed by one Employee.

Each entity is shown as a single table as shown in figure 2.17. To implement this relationship, we would add a Manager attribute to the Store table. The Manger attribute would then act as a foreign key referencing the primary key of Employee table. Remember that in a one-to-one binary relationship, the primary key from the mandatory side (Employee) is placed as a foreign key in the optional side (Store). By looking at Manager column of Store table in figure 2.17, we could say that Rob Anderson is the Manager of the store.

Employee

EmployeeId	FirstName	LastName
1	Andrew	Jackson
2	Rob	Anderson
3	Nancy	Wong

Store

StoreName	Address	Manager
ABC Computers	128 Lawrence Ave	2

Figure 2.17 An example of One-to-one binary relationship

Figure 2.18 shows a One-to-many binary relationship. This is an example of a customer placing an order relationship. To find the cardinality between the two entities you ask the following questions.

Question: One Customer Places how many Orders?
Answer: The minimum is 1 and the maximum is many.
Place 1 and Crow's foot (many) next to Order entity.
Question: One Order is Placed by how many Customers?
Answer: The minimum 1 and the maximum 1.
Place both 1's next to Employee entity.

Each entity is shown as a single table as shown in figure 2.19. Since the Order table is on the many side, the Order table would have the primary key of Customer table as a foreign key. *Remember that the Primary key moves to the many side.* By looking at CustomerId column in Order table, we could say Alan Hankok (CustomerId = 1) placed one order (OrderNo = 1) while all the rest of the orders (OrderNo = 2, 3, 4) are placed by Henry Chan (CustomerId = 2).

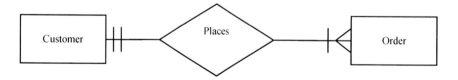

Figure 2.18 One-to-many binary relationship

Customer

CustomerId	CustFName	CustLName
1	Alan	Hankok
2	Henry	Chan

Order

OrderNo	OrderDate	CustomerId
1	10/1/2001	1
2	10/2/2001	2
3	10/3/2001	2
4	10/3/2001	2

Figure 2.19 One-to-many binary relationship

Figure 2.20 shows a Many-to-many binary relationship. This is an example of an order has products relationship. To find the cardinality between the two entities you ask the following questions.

From left to right, One Order has how many Products? The minimum is 1 and the maximum is many. Place 1 and crow foot next to Product entity.

From right to left, One Product can be in how many **Orders**? The minimum is zero and the maximum is many. Place 0 and crow foot next to Order entity.

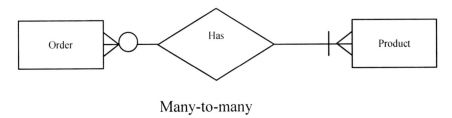

Many-to-many

Figure 2.20 Many-to-many binary relationship

By looking at this example, one would think that each entity would be converted into a table as we have done in the previous examples. But relational databases do not allow many-to-many relationship tables. To solve this problem, you should create a junction table that includes the primary keys from both tables and any additional columns that may be appropriate for a particular scenario. The relationship between the original tables and the new junction table is one-to-many. We call the new junction table as OrderProduct by combining the names of the two tables. You could give it any other name that may suit the situation. As the new junction table is on the many side of the relationship, the primary keys from both Order and Product tables would be included in OrderProduct table as foreign keys. Figure 2.21 shows this transformation using Crow's foot model.

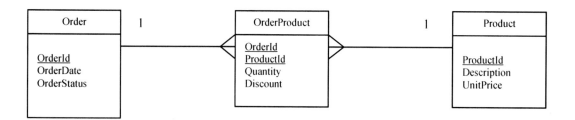

Figure 2.21 Converting a many-to-many relationship into two binary one-to-many relationships

Remember that you must make sure that the composite primary key is unique. There are times when the combination of the primary keys of the original entities does not make a unique key. In such a situation, you should either add another attribute to the primary key to make it unique or think of a new attribute to use as a primary key. In our example the combination key is unique. Figure 2.22 shows the equivalent tables to figure 2.21.

Order

OrderId	OrderDate	OrderStatus
O1	10/2/2003	Filled
O2	10/5/2003	Not filled

Product

ProductId	Description	UnitPrice
P1	CPU	$300
P2	Hard disk	$150
P3	Motherboard	$200

OrderProduct

OrderId	ProductId	Quantity	Discount
O1	P1	1	10%
O2	P1	1	20%
O3	P3	2	10%
O4	P2	1	10%

Figure 2.22 Resulting tables from splitting many-to-many binary relationship into two one-to-many binary relationships

Associative entity

In reality, an associative entity is a many-to-many relationship discussed in the previous topic. For the sake of explanation, this topic has been added so that the reader is aware of what an associative entity is in Chen's model. When the relationship between two entities is many-to-many and the relationship itself has attributes, this kind of situation suggest of converting the relationship into an entity called associative entity. The resulting associative entity has independent meaning and preferably can be identified with a single identifier attribute.

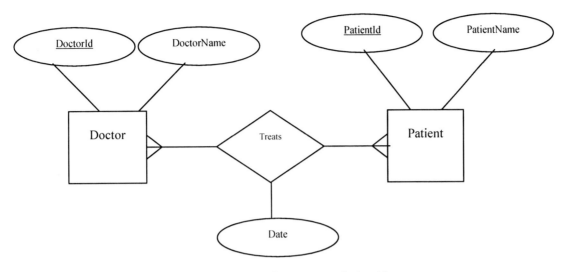

Figure 2.23 Attributes on a relationship

Consider two entities, Doctor and Patient as shown in figure 2.23. Treats is the relationship between them. A doctor can treat many patients and a patient can be treated by many doctors. The relationship between these two entities is many-to-many. What if the Treats relationship has attributes associated with it like treatment date. Generally attributes belong to an entity not to a relationship. This suggests of converting the relationship to an entity. Let us convert this relationship into an associative entity and we call this new entity Treatment as shown in figure 2.24(a).

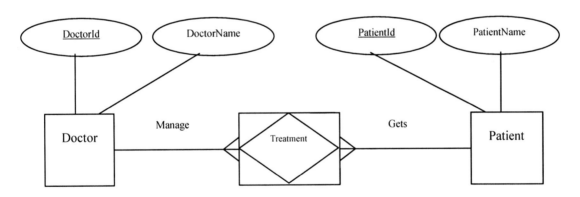

Figure 2.24 (a) An associative entity

As you can see in figure 2.24(a), by converting a relationship to an associative entity causes two changes. The relationship notation is boxed in an entity box which shows that it is an associative entity. Crow foot, which is a notation for many, now terminates at associative entity instead of at each participating entity.

To check the cardinality in the new entity relationship diagram, we ask our self the following questions.

Question: One Doctor Manages how many Treatments?
Answer: Zero or many.
Question: One Treatment can be Managed by how many Doctors?
Answer: One
Question: One Patient Gets how many Treatments?
Answer: Zero or many
Question: One Treatment is done to how many Patients?
Answer: One

The answer to our questions confirmed that the many relationship moved to the new associative entity.

The new Treatment entity in figure 2.24 (a) has an independent meaning. The default primary key for Treatment entity is the combination of the two primary keys DoctorId (from Doctor entity) and PatientId (from Patient entity). This default key does not uniquely identify a given treatment. A Patient may receive the same treatment from the same Doctor on more than one occasion. What if we include the treatment date as a part of the primary key? It would be fine if the same patient do not get more then one treatment on the same day but we can not guarantee that. To solve this problem we select a natural unique identifier (TreatmentNo) as a primary key as shown in figure 2.24(b).

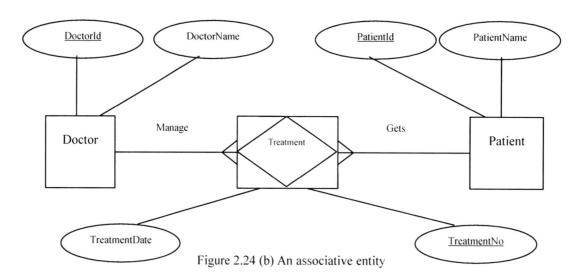

Figure 2.24 (b) An associative entity

Now each treatment can be uniquely identified by TreatmentNo. The two primary keys from Doctor and Patient entities still remain in Treatment table as foreign keys but not as part of the primary key. The TreatmentDate attribute would also be included in the Treatment table.

Let us represent figure 2.23 in its equivalent Crow's foot notations and then convert it to its equivalent tables as shown in figure 2.25

Converting the many-to-many relationship into two
one-to-many relationships

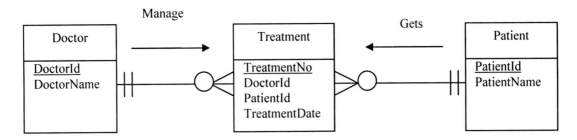

Doctor

DoctorId	DoctorName
D1	Tom Lam
D2	Carl Fu

Patient

PatientId	PatientName
P1	Robert Brown
P2	Mary Row

Treatment

TreatmentNo	DoctorId	PatientId	TreatmentDate
T1	D1	P1	2/5/2004
T2	D1	P1	2/5/2004
T3	D1	P2	2/6/2004
T4	D2	P1	2/9/2004

Figure 2.25 Converting many-to-many relationship to Associative entity

Ternary relationship

A relationship between the instances of three entity types is called Ternary relationship. A relationship between three or more entities is a complex relationship. Figure 2.26 shows an example of a ternary relationship.

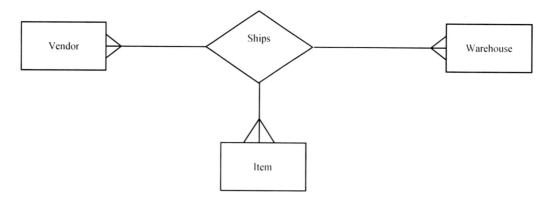

Figure 2.26 An example of a Ternary relationship

Ternary relationship is not the same as three binary relationships. Let us say that a **Vendor** *Ships* an **Item** to a **Warehouse**. There are three entity types involved in this situation, Vendor, Item and Warehouse. The relationship is Ships. A Vendor ships an Item. Where? To a Warehouse. A Vendor ships to a Warehouse. What? An Item. Each of these questions suggests that you can not talk about the relationship between two entities without considering the third entity. Looking at the cardinality between the three entities, we could say that each Vendor can ship many Items to any numbers of Warehouses. Each Item can be shipped by any number of vendors to any number of Warehouses. Each Warehouse could be shipped many Items by any number of Vendors.

What if you can ship an item by air, sea and land? This suggests that shipping method is an attribute of ships. Generally an attribute belongs to an entity not to a relationship. You can simplify this kind of relationship by introducing a new entity and defining binary relationships between each of the original entities and the new entity. In this example the ternary relationship type *Ships* (verb) can be replaced with an entity type Shipment (noun). Now a binary relationship between Shipment and each of the entity types Vendor, Item and Warehouse is born. The new entity is an associative entity and is shown in figure 2.27.

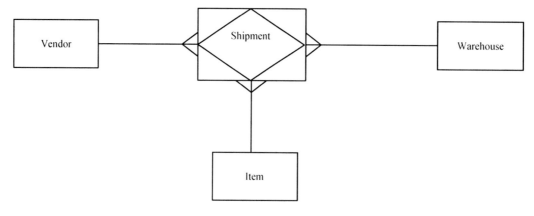

Figure 2.27

As we know that each entity is a table in relational model. Applying relational model to ternary relationship, each entity including the new entity becomes a single table. As Shipment is an associative entity, the three primary keys are included in the Shipment table. The combination of the three primary keys (VendorId, ItemId, WarehouseId) does not uniquely identify a shipment. Therefore we can not use this combination as a primary key. Let us combine these three attributes with ShipmentDate attribute to provide a unique identification. If there is more than one shipment on the same date then this combination would not work. Let us say that each shipment would have a number assigned to it. Now this number could easily identify any shipment. We call this number as ShipmentNo and add it as an attribute to Shipment table. We make this attribute as a primary key for the Shipment table. Now you can easily trace any shipment without the need of using any other attributes. Figure 2.28 shows the tables for figure 2.27.

Item

ItemId	Description	Cost
I1	Printer	$100
I2	Memory	$30
I3	Floppy drive	$20

Vendor

VendorId	VendorName
V1	Aki Computers
V2	North Computers

Warehouse

WarehouseId	City
W1	Chicago
W2	Boston

Shipment

ShipmentNo	ItemId	VendorId	WarehouseId	ShipmentMethod	DateShiped
S1	I1	V1	W1	Air	1/9/2004
S2	I1	V2	W1	Air	1/9/2004
S3	I2	V1	W1	Ground	1/13/2004
S4	I3	V1	W2	Air	1/14/2004

Figure 2.28 Converting a Ternary relationship to relational tables

Let us check the cardinality for figure 2.27 from the tables in figure 2.28.

From Item towards Shipment:
Let us name the new relationship from Item towards Shipment in figure 2.27 as **Is_in**.
Q: One Item **Is_in** how many Shipments?
By looking at ItmeId column in Shipment table, we notice that ItemId I1 (Printer) is in ShipmentNo S1 & S2. The answer to the above question is that the same item can be on many shipments. This suggests that the minimum cardinality is one and the maximum is

many. Place 1 for the minimum and a crow foot for the maximum next to the Shipment entity as shown in figure 2.29

From Shipment towards Item:

Let us name the relationship in the opposite direction as **Has**.

Q: One Shipment **Has** how many Items?

By looking at ShipmentNo column in Shipment table, we notice that for each ShipmentNo, there is only one ItemId associated with it. Remember that the ShipmentNo is a primary key for the shipment table and can not be repeated. This suggests that the cardinality from Shipment towards Item is the minimum of one and the maximum of one. Place 1 for the minimum and 1 for the maximum next to Item entity as shown in figure 2.29

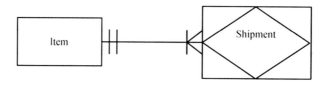

Figure 2.29

From Vendor towards Shipment:

Let us name the new relationship from Vendor towards Shipment as **Ships**.

Q: One Vendor **Ships** how many Shipments?

By looking at column VendorId in Shipment table, we notice that VendorId V1 Ships ShipmentNo S1, S3 & S4. The answer to the above question is that the same Vendor Ships many shipments. This suggests that the minimum cardinality is one and the maximum is many. Place 1 for the minimum and a crow foot for the maximum next to Shipment entity as shown in figure 2.30

From Shipment towards Vendor:

Let us name the relationship in the opposite direction as **Is_shipped**.

Q: One Shipment Is_shipped by how many Vendors?

By looking at ShipmentNo column in Shipment table, we notice that for each ShipmentNo, there is only one VendorId associated with it. Remember that the ShipmentNo is a primary key for the shipment table and can not be repeated. This suggests that the cardinality from Shipment towards Vendor is the minimum of one and the maximum of one. Place 1 for the minimum and 1 for the maximum next to Vendor entity as shown in figure 2.30

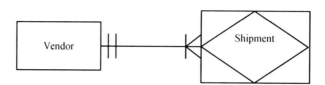

Figure 2.30

From Warehouse towards Shipment:
Let us name the new relationship from Warehouse towards Shipment as **Receives**.
Q: One Warehouse **Receives** how many Shipments?
By looking at WarehouseId column in Shipment table, we notice that WarehouseId W1 Receives ShipmentNo S1, S2 & S3. The answer to the above question is that the same warehouse can receive many shipments. This suggests that the minimum cardinality is one and the maximum is many. Place 1 for the minimum and a crow foot for the maximum next to Shipment entity as shown in figure 2.31.

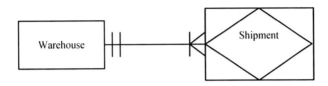

Figure 2.31

From Shipment towards Warehouse:
Let us name the relationship in the opposite direction as **Is_shipped**.
Q: One Shipment **Is_shipped** to how many Warehouses?
By looking at ShipmentNo column in Shipment table, we notice that for each ShipmentNo, there is only one WarehouseId associated with it. This suggests that the cardinality from Shipment towards Warehouse is the minimum of one and the maximum of one. Place 1 for the minimum and 1 for the maximum next to Warehouse entity as shown in figure 2.31

Specialization and Generalization

Consider the example of employees working for a company. The Employee entity has different attributes such as EmployeeId, Name, DateHired, HourlyRate, Salary, StockOption and CommissionRate. Figure 2.31 shows an Employee entity with its equivalent relational table.

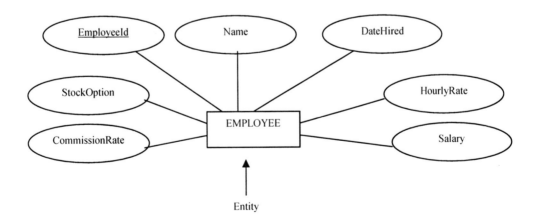

Employee

EmployeeId	Name	DateHired	HourlyRate	Salary	StockOption	CommissionRate
1	Alan	1/2/2000	$10			
2	Diana	3/4/1999		50,000	10%	
3	Larry	5/7/1996				5%
4	Norma	1/6/2001				5%

Figure 2.32 Employee entity with its equivalent relational table

By looking at the Employee table you would notice that the first three columns are filled up but the other four columns (HourlyRate, Salary, StockOption & commissionRate) have many empty spaces or in other words has a lot of nulls. Although all the workers are employees and they share some attributes but there are some attributes that they do not share. Some employees work on salary, some on commission and some on hourly rate. To minimize the number of nulls, we introduce the concept of entity supertype and subtype.

A supertype (parent) entity contains the shared attributes while the subtype (children) entity contains the unique attributes. A subtype entity inherits its attributes and its relationships from the supertype entity. The property by which subtype entities inherit values of all attributes of the supertype is called **Attribute inheritance**. This property makes it unnecessary to include supertype attributes redundantly with the subtypes. The relationship between a subtype and a supertype is known as **ISA**. An Hourly employee **IS An** employee. Because the relationship name (ISA) is always the same, it is not shown on the diagram. The relationship between supertype and subtypes is 1:1. Figure 2.33 shows the conversion of Employee entity into a supertype (Employee) entity and three subtype entities (Hourly, Salaried and Commission).

When we identify a subtype of an entity, we associate the attributes specific to the subtype and also identify any relationships between the subtype and other entities or subtypes. This process of maximizing the difference between members of an entity by identifying their distinguishing characteristics is called **Specialization**. Specialization is a top down approach to defining a set of subtypes and their related subtypes. We would say that Hourly, Salaried and Commission are specialized subtypes of Employee supertype.

When we attempt to identify the similarities between subtypes such as common attributes and relationships, this process is called **Generalization**. The process of generalization is a bottom up approach, which results in the identification of a generalized supertype from the original subtypes. We would say that Hourly, Salaried and Commision are specialized subtypes of Employee Supertype. Where EmployeeId, Name and DateHired are the attributes of a generalized Employee supertype.

The basic notations that we use for supertype/subtype relationship are shown in figure 2.33. The supertype is connected with a line to a circle, which in turn is connected by a line to each subtype that has been defined. The V shaped symbol on each line connecting a subtype to the circle indicates that the subtype is a subset of the supertype. It also indicates the direction of the supertype/subtype relationship.

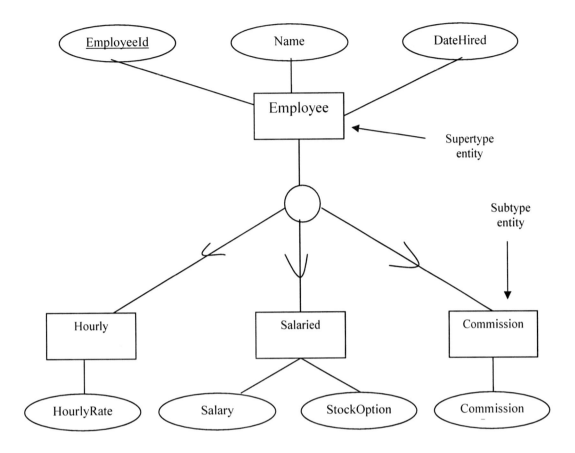

Figure 2.33 Supertype/Subtype entities

There are two constraints that apply to supertype/subtype relationship called completeness and disjointness. **Completeness constraint** determines whether every entity of a supertype is an entity in one of the subtypes. Completeness constraint is further subdivided into two rules: Total specialization rule and Partial specialization rule.

Total Specialization

Total specialization rule specifies that a member of a supertype must be a member of at least one subtype. Total specialization is indicated by a double line extending from the supertype to the circle. Let us say that an employee must be paid in (at least one of) the form of Hourly, Salaried or Commission. This is our business rule. A double line is drawn from Employee entity to the circle as shown in figure 2.34.

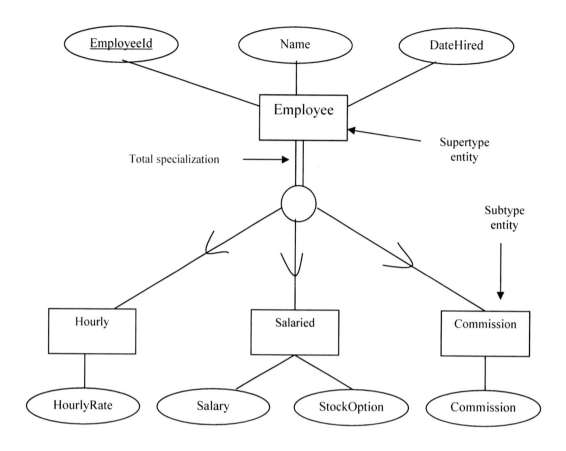

Figure 2.34 Supertype/Subtype of Employee entity

Partial Specialization

Partial specialization rule specifies that a member of a supertype does not have to belong to any of its subtypes. To represent partial specialization, a single line is drawn from supertype to the circle. Consider the example of a Vehicle as shown in figure 2.35. Car and Bus are its subtypes. A vehicle has to be a Car or a Bus. What if the vehicle is a motorbike? This is neither a car and nor a bus but has all the attributes of a vehicle. This is an example of partial specialization. The single line from Vehicle entity to the circle shows that a vehicle doesn't have to be a Car or a Bus.

So far we have discussed completeness constraint rules. The second constraint that apply to supertype/subtype is disjointness constraint. **Disjointness constraint** determines whether subtypes do have any entities in common. A disjointness constraint only applies when a supertype has more than one subtype. Disjointness constraint is further subdivided into two: Disjoint rule and Overlap rule.

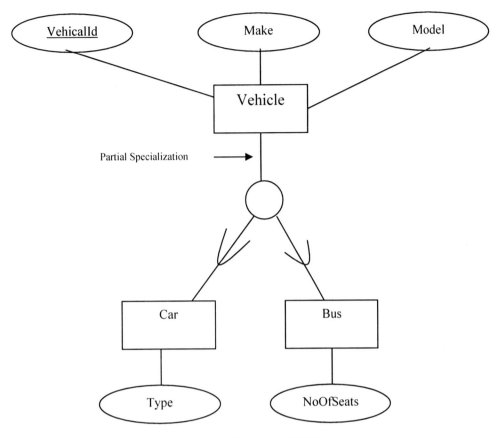

Figure 2.35 Supertype/Subtype of Vehicle entity

Disjoint Rule

Disjoint rule specifies that if a supertype is a member of one subtype, it can not be a member of another subtype. Let us say that our business rule states that at any time an employee can be paid through only one method (either Hourly, Salary or Commission). This is a disjoint rule. The disjoint rule is specified by placing the letter 'd' in the circle. Applying the disjoint rule to figure 2.34, makes it look as shown in figure 2.36.

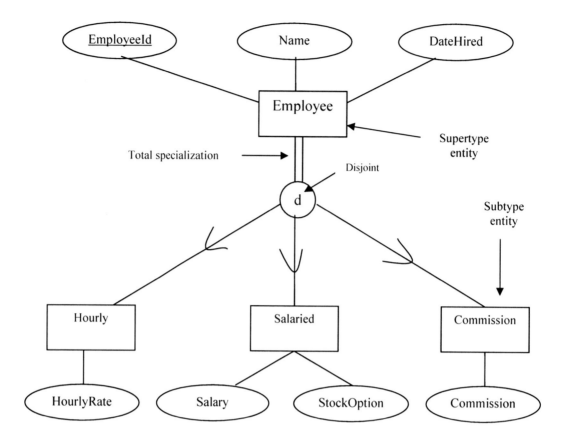

Figure 2.36 Supertype/Subtype of Employee entity

Overlap Rule

Overlap rule specifies that a supertype can be a member of two or more subtypes. Consider a business rule for figure 2.34 which states that at any time an employee can be paid in any form (Hourly, Salary or Commission). This is an overlap rule as an employee can be paid in more than one form. The overlap rule is specified by placing the letter 'o' in the circle. Applying the overlap rule to figure 2.34, makes it look as shown in figure 2.37.

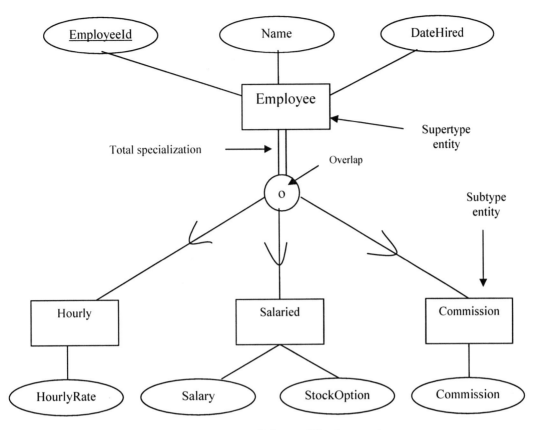

Figure 2.37 Supertype/Subtype of Employee entity

Coming back to our discussion of Employee table in figure 2.32, the main purpose of discussing specialization/generalization is to help us create tables for such situations and minimize the number of nulls. Consider the business rule that an employee must be paid through one of the given methods which are Salary, Hourly or Commission. Applying this condition to table 2.32 would give us figure 2.36. The relationship that the Employee supertype has with it subtypes (Hourly, Salaried & Commission) is totally specialized. Each member of the Employee supertype must belong to one of the subtypes represented by the double lines.

The other condition that is applied to this relationship is that a member of the Employee supertype can belong to only one subtype. In other words, the subtypes do not have any entities in common. This relationship is disjoint and represented by 'd'.

Once you identify a supertype entity and subtype entities, there are various options of representing such a relationship. The selection of the most appropriate option is dependent on completeness and disjointness constraints on supertype/subtype relationship. Table 2.1 provide some guidelines for how best to represent a supertype/subtype relationship.

Completeness constraint	Disjointness constraint	Tables required
Total specialization	Overlap	Single table
Partial specialization	Overlap	Two tables: one table for supertype and one table for all subtypes
Total specialization	Disjoint	Many tables: one table for each combined supertype/subtype
Partial specialization	Disjoint	Many tables: one table for supertype and one for each subtype

Table 2.1

Looking at table 2.1 one can conclude that the best solution to represent the Employee supertype/subtype relationship in figure 2.36 is to create a separate table for each combined supertype/subtype. As there is one supertype and three subtypes, combining the supertype with each subtype would result in three tables as shown in figure 2.38. The EmployeeId is the primary key for each combined table.

Hourly

EmployeeId	Name	DateHired	HourlyRate
1	Alan	1/2/2000	$10

Salaried

EmployeeId	Name	DateHired	Salary	StockOption
2	Diana	3/4/1999	50,000	10%

Commission

EmployeeId	Name	DateHired	CommissionRate
3	Larry	5/7/1996	5%
4	Norma	1/6/2001	5%

Figure 2.38

By looking at figure 2.38, we could say that all null values in Employee table in figure 2.32 have been removed by applying specialization/generalization.

Let us have another look at the relationship in figure 2.35 between the supertype (Vehicle) and subtypes (Car & Bus). A vehicle can be a Car or a Bus. If a vehicle is a motorbike then it is neither a Car nor a Bus but has all the attributes of a vehicle. This is a partially specialized relationship. Can a vehicle be a Car and a Bus at the same time? The answer is no. Therefore, the relationship is disjoint. You can write **d** with in the circle to show that the relationship is disjoint. Now looking at table 2.1, one can conclude that the best solution to represent Vehicle supertype/subtype relationship is to create one table for supertype and one for each subtype as shown in figure 2.39. The primary keys (CarId & BusId) references the primary key VehicleId.

Vehicle

VehicalId	Make	Model
1	Yamaha	MB100
2	Honda	Prelude
3	Toyota	Coaster

Car

CarId	Type
2	Sports

Bus

BusId	NoOfSeats
3	20

Figure 2.39

The relationship between supertype (Employee) and subtypes (Hourly, Salaried & Commission) in figure 2.37 is totally specialized and overlapped. Looking at table 2.1 one can conclude that the best solution to represent Employee supertype/subtype relationship is to create a single table for all. This means that for this situation we should leave the table in figure 2.32 in its current condition.

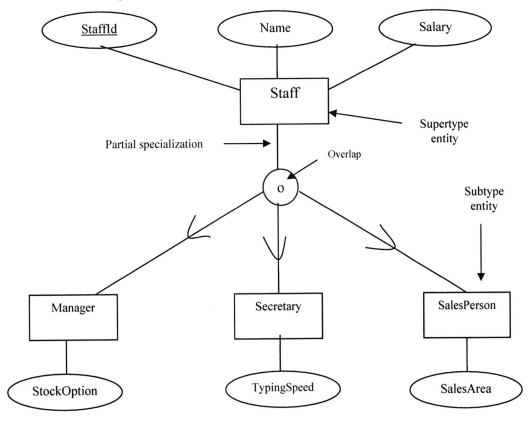

Figure 2.40 Supertype/Subtype of Staff entity

Consider the relationship between Supertype (Staff) and subtypes (Manager, Salesperson & Secretary) in figure 2.40. A member of staff may not be a Manager, Salesperson or a Secretary. This is partial specialization. What if a member of a staff can belong to more than one subtypes. This is an overlape rule. In such a situation, table 2.1 suggest of creating two tables. One table for supertype and one table for all subtypes as shown in figure 2.41. The primary key (StaffSubtypeId) references the primary key (StaffId).

Staff

StaffId	Name	Salary
1	Alex	50,000
2	Carl	40,000
3	Jody	30,000

StaffSubtype

StaffSubtypeId	StockOptions	TypingSpeed	SalesArea
1	10%		
2	5%		North York
3		80 Words/min	Markham

Figure 2.41

Creating Tables from ER Diagram

The relational data model represents data in the form of tables. The term 'relation' is just a mathematical term for a table. However, not all tables are relations. Relations have some specific properties that distinguish them from non relational table. These properties are

- Each relation has a unique name in a database
- Each row is unique.
- Each column (attribute) in a relation has a unique name
- A relation can not have multi valued attributes

From now on, when we say of a table, that means a table with relational properties. There are two common methods of expressing a schema for a database.

Text Method

For each entity write down the entity name, followed by its attributes in parentheses. The primary key attribute is underlined.
Employee (EmployeeId, FirstName, LastName).

Graphical Method

For a graphical representation, each entity is represented by a rectangle containing the attributes. The primary key is underlined.

Employee

EmployeeId	FirstName	LastName

The text method has the advantage of simplicity. The graphical method provides a better way of expressing the referential integrity. Creating tables from ER diagram is a straight forward process with a well defined set of rules.

Mapping entities

Each strong entity in an ERD is converted into a table. Each table is given the same name as the entity and each attribute in the ERD is shown as a column in the table. The identifier attribute becomes a primary key of the table and is underlined. Figure 2.42 shows the mapping of Employee entity into its relational table.

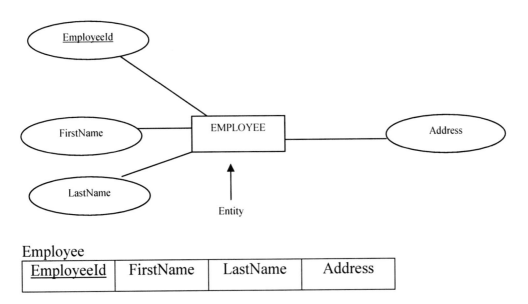

Employee

EmployeeId	FirstName	LastName	Address

Figure 2.42 Mapping an entity to its graphical representation

The address attribute in Employee entity is a composite attribute. It can be broken into components parts like Street, City, State and PostalCode. When an entity has composite attribute, only the simple component attributes of the composite attribute are included in the new table. Figure 2.43 shows the new mapping.

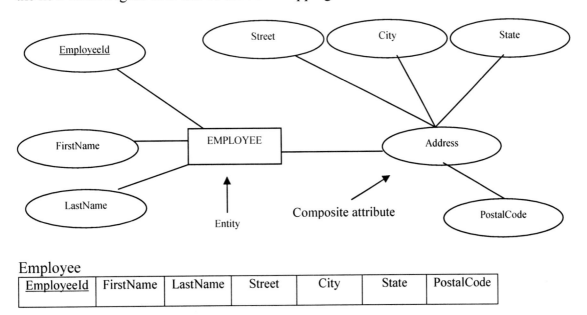

Employee

EmployeeId	FirstName	LastName	Street	City	State	PostalCode

Figure 2.43 Mapping an Entity with Composite attributes

38

Consider the Employee entity has a PhoneNo attribute. Let us assume that an Employee can have many phone numbers. Now the PhoneNo attribute is a multivalued attribute. When an entity contains a multivalued attribute, you have to create two new tables. The first table contains all the attributes of the entity except the multivalued attribute. The second table contains two attributes. The first of these attributes is the primary key from the first table. The second is the multivalued attribute. Both of these attributes form the primary key for the second table. When a primary key consist of more than one attribute, then it is called a composite key. The primary key from the first table (Employee) in the second table (EmployeePhNo) is called a foreign key. Figure 2.44 shows the transformation of an entity with multivalued attributes into two tables

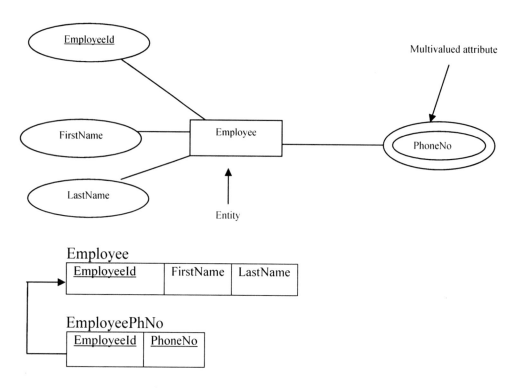

Figure 2.44 Mapping an entity with multivalued attributes

Mapping weak entities

Consider an employee has dependents. The Employee is a strong entity where the Dependent is a weak entity. The Dependent entity depends on the existence of Employee entity. The relationship between Employee and Dependent is 'has'. A weak entity does not have an attribute which could be a complete identifier. Therefore, it must have an attribute which can distinguish the various occurrences of the weak entity. This attribute is called a partial identifier.

For each weak entity (Dependent) create a new table and include all the attributes in the table. Include the primary key of the owner entity (Employee) as a foreign key attribute in the new table. The primary key of the new table is a combination of the primary key of the owner (EmployeeId) and the partial identifier of the weak entity (DepdFirstName, DepdLastName). Figure 2.45 shows the mapping of a weak entity into tables.

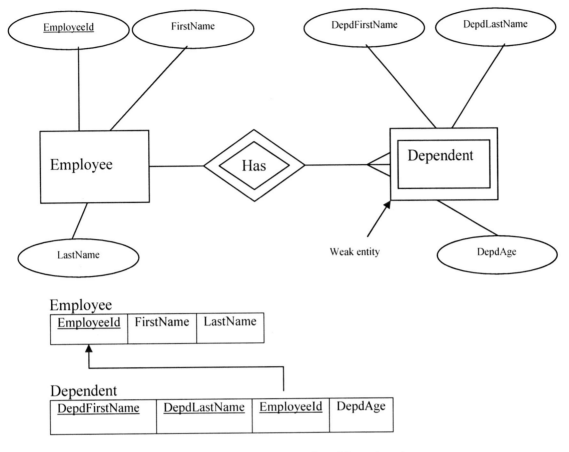

Figure 2.45 Mapping an entity with weak entity

Mapping Unary relationships

A relationship between the instances of a Single entity type is a Unary relationship. The two most common types of Unary relationships are one-to-many and many-to-many. In case of one-to-many Unary relationship, each entity is mapped to a table. Then with in the same table a foreign key attribute is added referencing the primary key. This key is also called recursive foreign key. Consider the example of an Employee (single instance of an entity) Supervise other Employee (many instances of an entity). This is a one-to-many relationship. Applying the stated rules will result in Figure 2.46. SupervisorId is the recursive foreign key.

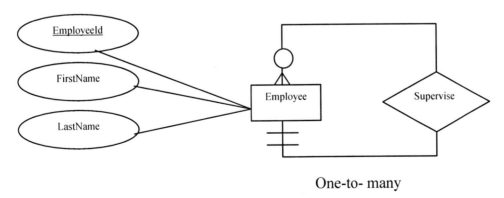

One-to- many

Employee

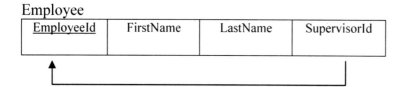

EmployeeId	FirstName	LastName	SupervisorId

Figure 2.46 Mapping a one-to-many Unary relationship to its equivalent tables

Consider the example of taking a Course. This is a many-to-many unary relationship. A course could require 0 or many courses before starting the course. On the other hand the same course could be part of a requirement for 0 or many other courses.

In case of many-to-many unary relationship, two tables are created. One has to represent the entity and the other to represent the many-to-many associative relationship with itself. The primary key in the second table consist of two attributes (CourseNo, RequirementNo). Both of these attributes takes their values from the primary key of the first table. Any non key attributes are also included in the second table. Figure 2.47 shows the mapping of many-to-many unary relationship

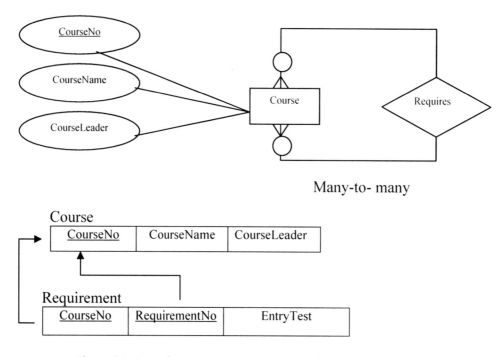

Many-to- many

Course

CourseNo	CourseName	CourseLeader

Requirement

CourseNo	RequirementNo	EntryTest

Figure 2.47 Mapping a many-to-many unary relationship to its equivalent tables

Mapping Binary relationships

A relationship between the instances of two entity types is called Binary relationship. This is the most common type of relationship. A binary relationship can be one-to-one, one-to-many and many-to-many.

Mapping one-to-one binary relationship

Consider a one-to-one binary relationship of an Employee Managing a Store. The association from the Employee to Store is an optional one since an employee may or may not manage a store. The association from the Store to Employee is a mandatory one since each store must be managed by one employee. In this situation Employee entity is the mandatory side while the Store entity is the optional side. Mapping a binary one-to-one relationship requires two tables, one for each participating entity. The primary key from the mandatory side table is included as a foreign key in the optional side table. Figure 2.48 shows the mapping of one-to-one binary relationship.

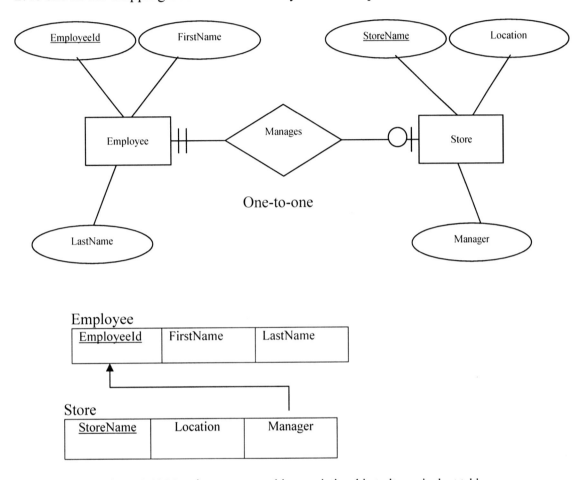

Figure 2.48 Mapping one-to-one binary relationship to its equivalent tables

Mapping one-to-many binary relationship

Mapping one-to-many binary relationship involves the creation of two tables, each one representing each participating entity. The primary key of the table on the one side is included in the table on the many side as a foreign key. Consider the situation of Customer Placing an Order. A Customer can Place many Orders. Each Order is Placed by one Customer. This is a one-to-many relationship. In this situation, the Customer table is the one side table and the Order table is the many side table. The primary key (CustomerId) from the Customer table (one side) is included as a foreign key in the Order table (many side). Figure 2.49 shows the mapping of a one-to-many binary relationship to tables.

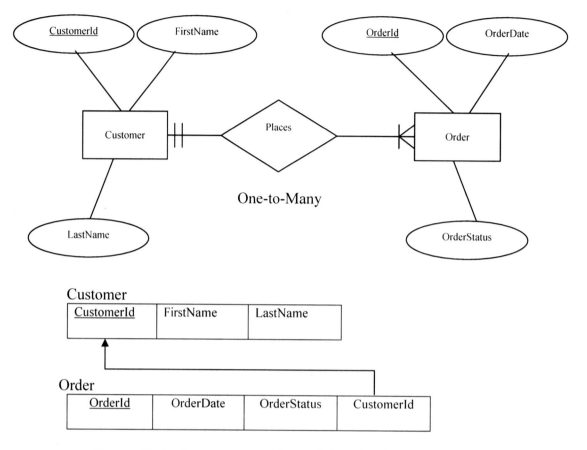

One-to-Many

Customer

CustomerId	FirstName	LastName

Order

OrderId	OrderDate	OrderStatus	CustomerId

Figure 2.49 Mapping one-to-many binary relationship to its equivalent tables

Mapping many-to-many binary relationship

Mapping a binary Many-to-many relationship requires three tables, one for each participating entity and a third one as a junction table. The junction table includes the primary keys from both tables. Any non key attributes that are associated with the many-to-many relationship are also included in the junction table. The two primary key attributes becomes a primary key for the junction table. Make sure the composite key is unique. In case the combination of the two primary keys is not a unique key, you must add another attribute from the junction table to the primary key to make it unique or use another attribute as a primary key.

Consider the example of a customer has an account. Let us make the assumption that a customer can have many accounts and an account can be shared by many customers. This is a many-to-many binary relationship. In this situation we would create three tables, one table for each participating entity and a third one as a junction table. We call the junction table as CustomerAccount and it would include the primary keys from the two tables. The combination of these two primary keys provides a unique key. Figure 2.50 shows the mapping of many-to-many binary relationship to its equivalent tables.

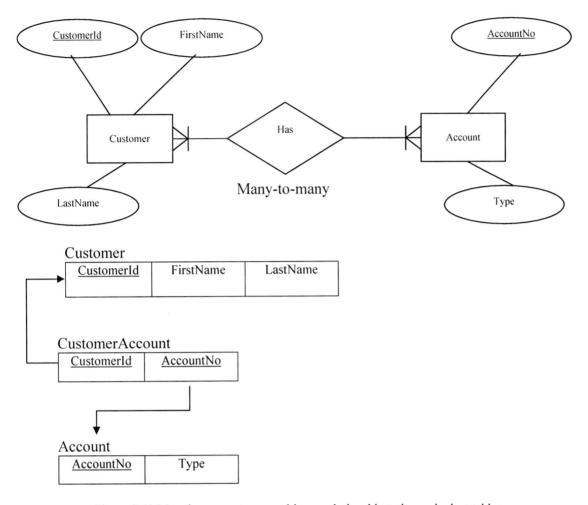

Figure 2.50 Mapping many-to-many binary relationship to its equivalent tables

Mapping Associative relationship

An associative entity is a form of many-to-many binary relationship. It depends whether an identifier was assigned to the associative entity or not.

Identifier not assigned

If an identifier was not assigned then mapping an associative relationship to tables is almost the same as mapping a binary many-to-many relationship. You start by creating one table for each participating entity and the third one for the associative entity. The default primary key for the associative table consists of the two primary keys from the other two tables. To see this situation, you could refer to the already described example in figure 2.50. In this situation the default composite primary key is unique.

The other case is when an identifier is not assigned but the default composite primary key is not unique. Consider two entities, Client and Property. Views is the relationship between the two entities. A Client can View several Properties and a Property can be Viewed by several Clients. The relationship between these two entities is many-to-many. As Views has its own attributes like InspectionDate, Comments, we can convert this relationship to an associative entity and call it Inspection entity as shown in figure 2.51(a)

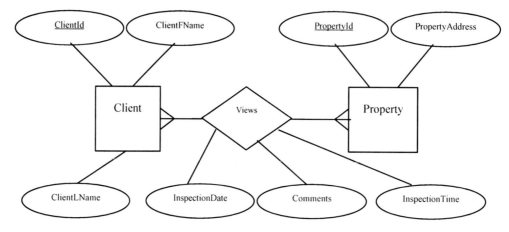

Attributes on a relationship

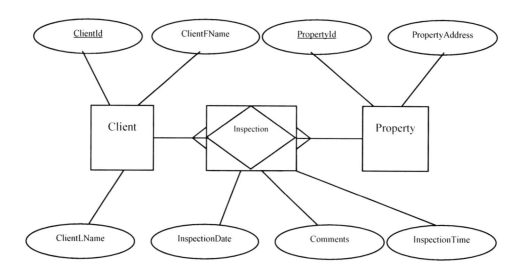

Figure 2.51 (a) An associative entity

Mapping the relationship in figure 2.51 (a) involves the creation of three tables, one for each participating entities and the third one for the associative entity. The primary key from the two tables are included in the Inspection table. The default composite key does not uniquely identify instances of the associative entity as the same client may view the same property many times. Let us combine the default primary key with InspectionDate to get a primary key. What happen if the client inspects the same property twice on the same day. This also doesn't give a unique key. To resolve this issue add InspectionTime as part of the primary key. Now the new primary key consists of four attributes, ClientId, PropertyId, InspectionDate and InspectionTime. This composite key can uniquely identify instances of the associative entity. Figure 2.51(b) shows the mapping of an associative entity into tables.

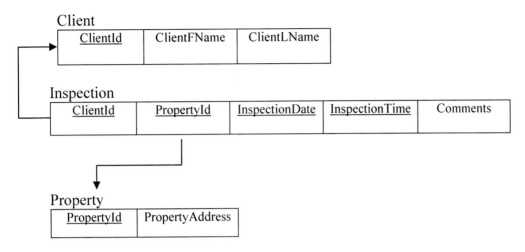

Figure 2.51(b) Mapping of an associative relationship without an assigned identifier to tables

Identifier assigned

Consider the example of a Customer Gets a Newspaper. A customer can get many newspapers. The same newspaper can be delivered to many customers. The relationship between Customer and Newspaper is many-to-many. The relationship Gets has its own attribute such as date as shown in figure 2.52.

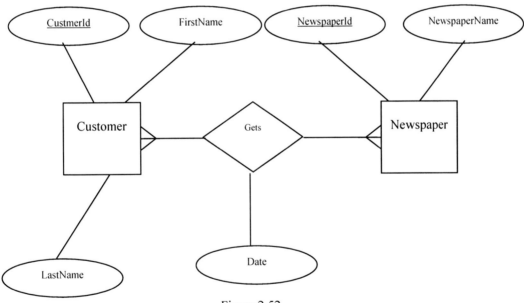

Figure 2.52

 We can convert the Gets relationship to an associative entity called Delivery as shown in figure 2.53. Applying the many-to-many mapping rule, we would get three tables, one for each participating entity and the third one for the associative entity. The default primary key for the Delivery table would be the combination of the primary keys from both participating tables. This default primary key can not uniquely identify the instances of Delivery. If we include the attribute Date, still this wouldn't guarantee uniqueness. A Customer may be getting a delivery of the newspaper in the morning (morning issue) and a delivery in the evening (evening issue). Now we would look for any natural identifier that would help us uniquely identify the instances of Delivery. Consider we choose DeliveryNo as identifier. This is a natural unique identifier and is familiar to users. In this situation DeliveryNo would become a primary key for the Delivery table and the other two primary keys from the participating tables become foreign keys in Delivery table. Date would become a non key attribute of Delivery table. Figure 2.53 shows the mapping of an associative relationship with an assigned identifier to its equivalent tables.

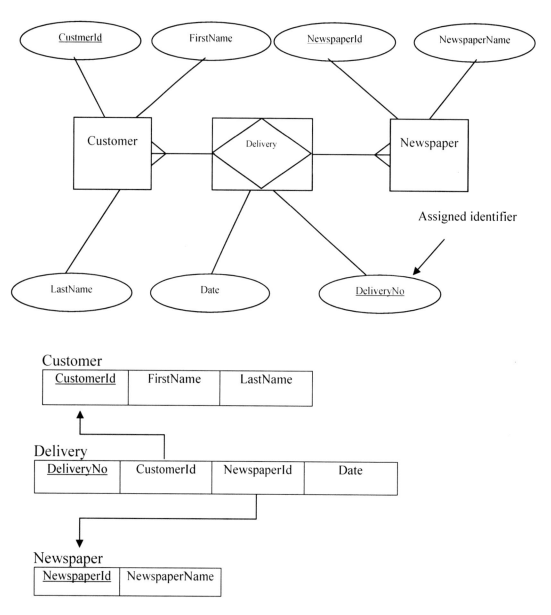

Figure 2.53 Mapping of an associative relationship with an assigned identifier to tables

Mapping Ternary relationships

Consider the example of a Teacher Recommends a certain Book on a certain Course. This is a ternary relationship. Converting the Recommends relationship to an associative relationship would give us the Recommendation associative entity.

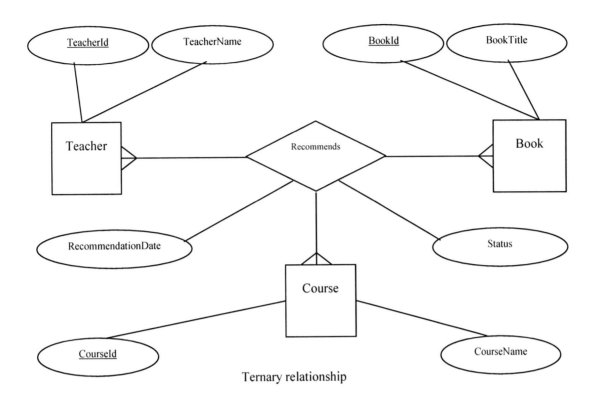

Ternary relationship

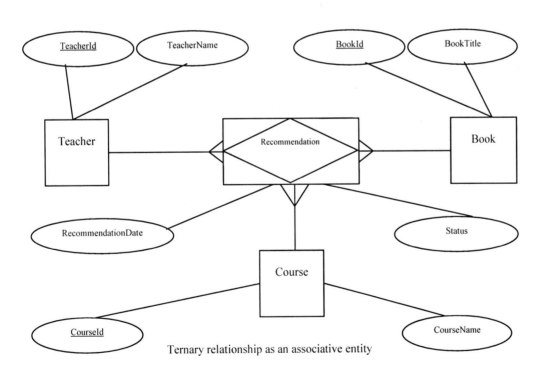

Ternary relationship as an associative entity

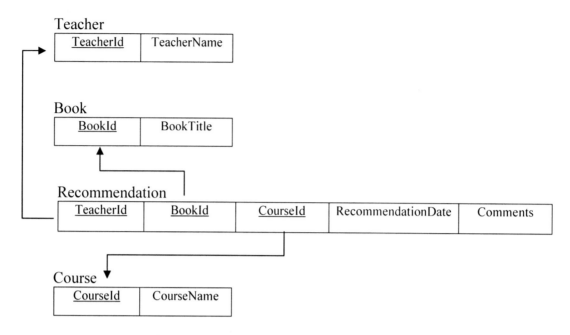

Figure 2.54 Mapping of a Ternary relationship to tables

Mapping this relationship involves the creation of four tables, one for each participating entity and the fourth one for the associative entity. The default primary key for the Recommendation table would be the combination of the primary keys from all three participating tables. This default primary key can uniquely identify the instances of Recommendation. Any non key attributes of the Recommendation entity becomes a part of the Recommendation table. If the composite key doesn't provide a unique key, additional attributes will be required to form a unique primary key. Figure 2.54 shows the mapping of a Ternary relationship into its equivalent tables.

Mapping Supertype/Subtype relationships

For each supertype/subtype relationship, you identify the supertype as parent entity and the subtype as child entity. Once you identify a supertype entity and subtype entities, there are various options of representing such a relationship. The selection of the most appropriate option is dependent on completeness and disjointness constraints on supertype/subtype relationship. Each subtype inherits the primary key from the supertype. Table 2.2 (a repeat of table 2.1) provides some guidelines for how best to represent a supertype/subtype relationship.

Completeness constraint	Disjointness constraint	Tables required
Total specialization	Overlap	Single table
Partial specialization	Overlap	Two tables: one table for supertype and one table for all subtypes
Total specialization	Disjoint	Many tables: one table for each combined supertype/subtype
Partial specialization	Disjoint	Many tables: one table for supertype and one for each subtype

Table 2.2

Consider the example in figure 2.55. The relationship between supertype and subtypes is totally specialized and disjoint. In this situation, Table 2.2 suggests of creating many tables, one for each combined supertype/subtype. Figure 2.56 shows the mapping of this relationship.

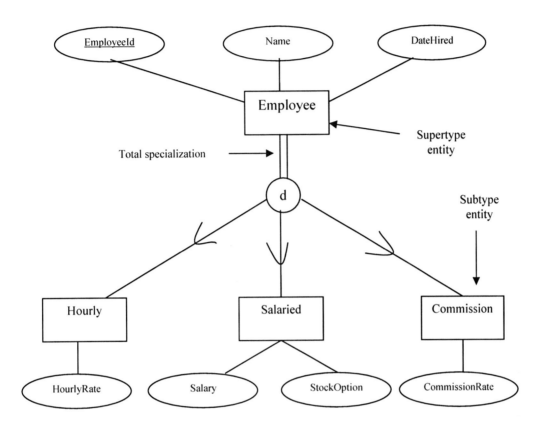

Figure 2.55 Supertype/Subtype of Employee entity

Hourly

EmployeeId	Name	DateHired	HourlyRate

Salaried

EmployeeId	Name	DateHired	Salary	StockOption

Commission

EmployeeId	Name	DateHired	CommissionRate

Figure 2.56 Mapping a totally specialized and disjoint relationship

Consider the example in figure 2.57. In this situation the relationship between supertype and subtypes is partially specialized and disjoint. In this case, Table 2.2 suggests of creating many tables, one table for supertype and one for each subtype. Figure 2.58 shows the mapping for this relationship.

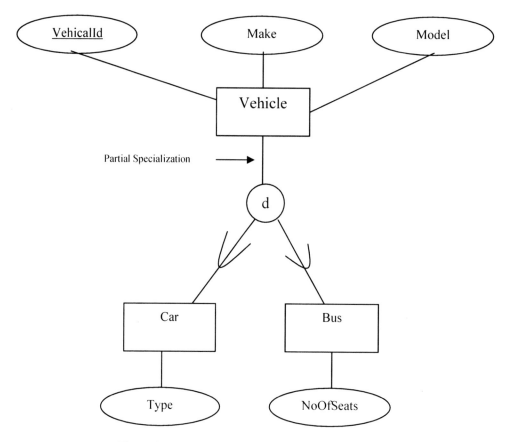

Figure 2.57 Supertype/Subtype of Vehicle entity

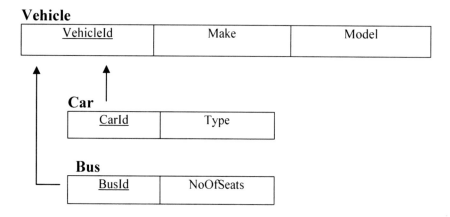

Figure 2.58 Mapping a partially specialized and disjoint relationship

Consider the example in figure 2.59. In this situation the relationship between supertype and subtypes is partially specialized and overlapped. In this case, Table 2.2 suggests of creating two tables, one table for supertype and one table for all combined subtypes. Figure 2.60 shows the mapping for this relationship.

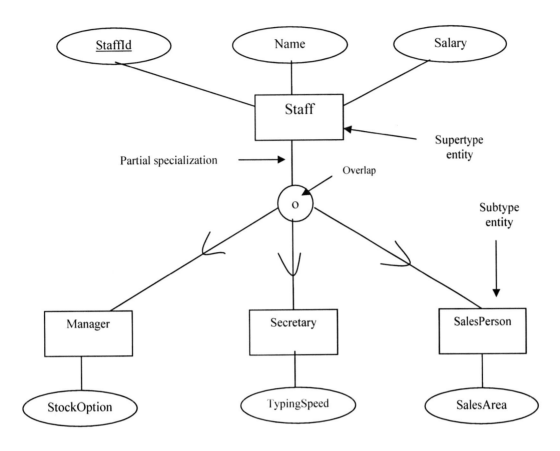

Figure 2.59 Supertype/Subtype of Employee entity

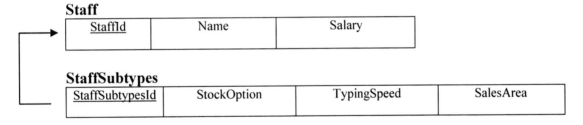

Figure 2.60 Mapping a partially specialized and overlapped relationship

This concludes our discussion on Entity relationship model. The concept of entities and relationships is fundamental to the process of database design. This chapter will help us in understanding the theory behind the design of a relational database.

Chapter 3

Normalization and Integrity Rules

Normalization works hand in hand with Data integrity rules. Normalization rules help you decide where to store units of data. Integrity rules help you identify units of data in order to protect the data. When you design a database, you should not pack every piece of data you run across into the nearest table. Just because your table for customers includes first name and last name fields does not mean you should put employees into the same table. Employees and Customers are two different entities that belong in two different places. There are many different normal forms. In this chapter, we will be discussing the first three normal forms as they are the most important.

Normalizing data

Data is stored in tables and tables contain columns where individual data items are stored. How do you figure out which piece of data belongs in which table, and how do you decide how many tables to create? Normalization is the process of structuring a database for efficiency by applying some common sense rules to organize it. Consider cloths in your laundry basket. You would never pick out articles of clothing at random and shove them into the closet. There should be a place for everything and everything should be in its place. If you keep your socks in multiple random places, you would never find a matching pair to wear in the morning for work. Normalization is the process of taking a tangled mass of data and untangling it, to make tables with logical places for each strand of the tangle. Normalization's end result is to help you develop a database with the following characteristics

- Each table must have a primary key
- All fields must contain atomic data
- There must be no repeating fields
- Each table must contain information about a single type of entity
- Each field in a table must depend on the entire primary key
- All non-key fields must be mutually independent

In order to normalize data you need an understanding of functional dependency.

Functional dependency

A dependency is when the value of one attribute is dependent on the value of another attribute. If you now the length and width of an area, you can calculate the area

Area = Length * Width

We can say that Area is functionally dependent on length and width. In databases we are more concerned with the functional dependencies between fields.

A functional dependency is a relationship of one attribute or field in a record to another. Suppose a company assigned each employee a unique employee number. Each employee has a number and a name. Two different employees may have the same name but their employee numbers would always be different and unique because the company defined them that way. It would be inconsistent in the database if there were two occurrences of the same employee number with different names. The idea of a functional dependency is to define one field as an anchor from which one can always find a single value for another field.

We write a functional dependency (FD) connection with an arrow:

EmployeeNo → Name

The expression EmployeeNo → Name is read as "EmployeeNo defines name" or "EmployeeNo implies Name"

We can conclude from the above discussion that

- Name is functionally dependent on EmployeeNo
- EmployeeNo functionally determines Name
- EmployeeNo is the determinant

The relationship is one way and you can not say that EmployeeNo is functionally dependent on Name. Two different employees may have the same name but their employee numbers would always be different and unique. It would be inconsistent in the database if there were two occurrences of the same employee number with different names. The attribute on the left hand side of the arrow in a functional dependency is called a determinant.

Consider table 3.1. A functional dependency diagram for this table is shown in figure 3.1. The functional dependencies in figure 3.1 indicate that the combination of CustomerId and NewspaperId is the only candidate key. This candidate key becomes the primary key or the determinant. In this case the primary key is a composite key. You would notice that DateDelivered is the only attribute that is functionally dependent on the full primary key consisting of the attributes CustomerId and NewspaperId. On the other hand, FirstName and LastName depend on part of the composite primary key which is CustomerId. NewspaperName and Price are also dependent on the part of the primary key which is NewspaperId. Dependencies based on only part of a composite primary key are called **Partial dependencies**.

CustomerId	FirstName	LastName	NewspaperId	NewspaperName	Price	DateDelivered
1	Alex	Wong	1	Chicago Mirror	$1.00	1/1/2001
1	Alex	Wong	2	Chicago Age	$1.50	1/1/2001
1	Alex	Wong	3	Chicago Sun	$2.00	1/2/2001
2	Jim	Chiu	2	Chicago Age	$1.50	1/5/2001
2	Jim	Chiu	3	Chicago Sun	$2.00	1/7/2001
3	Colleen	Woodburn	1	Chicago Mirror	$1.00	1/1/2001
3	Colleen	Woodburn	2	Chicago Age	$1.50	1/1/2001
3	Colleen	Woodburn	3	Chicago Sun	$2.00	1/5/2001

Table 3.1

If you pay close attention to the price attribute, you would notice that it is also dependent on the non-key attribute NewspaperName. Customers are charged different Prices for different newspapers. This condition is called transitive dependency. Functional dependency between two or more non-key attributes is called **Transitive dependency**. Any attribute that is a part of a primary key is called a key attribute. As the primary key is composed of two attributes, therefore, we have two key attributes which are CustomerId and NewspaperId.

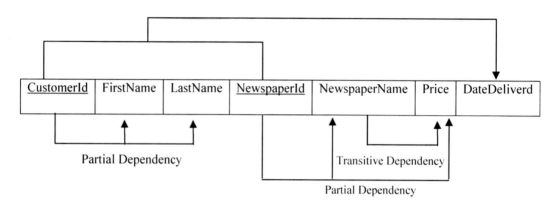

Figure 3.1

The dependencies in figure 3.1 can be written as following

CustomerId, NewspaperId → DateDelivered

CustomerId → FirstName, LastName

NewspaperId → NewspaperName, Price

NewpaperName → Price

First Normal Form

A relational table is in first normal form if all of the data values are atomic. For every row, there must exist only one value, not an array of values. Consider table 3.2. This table is not in first normal form as for every row, there exist an array of values.

CustomerId	FirstName	LastName	NewsPaperId	NewspaperName	Price	DateDelivered
1	Alex	Wong	1	Chicago Mirror	$1.00	1/1/2001
			2	Chicago Age	$1.50	1/1/2001
			3	Chicago Sun	$2.00	1/2/2001
2	Jim	Chiu	2	Chicago Age	$1.50	1/5/2001
			3	Chicago Sun	$2.00	1/7/2001
3	Colleen	Woodburn	1	Chicago Mirror	$1.00	1/1/2001
			2	Chicago Age	$1.50	1/1/2001
			3	Chicago Sun	$2.00	1/5/2001

Table 3.2

Converting table 3.2 to first normal form would give us table 3.3. As you can see, all multi valued attributes has been removed. Each row has one value.

CustomerId	FirstName	LastName	NewspaperId	NewspaperName	Price	DateDelivered
1	Alex	Wong	1	Chicago Mirror	$1.00	1/1/2001
1	Alex	Wong	2	Chicago Age	$1.50	1/1/2001
1	Alex	Wong	3	Chicago Sun	$2.00	1/2/2001
2	Jim	Chiu	2	Chicago Age	$1.50	1/5/2001
2	Jim	Chiu	3	Chicago Sun	$2.00	1/7/2001
3	Colleen	Woodburn	1	Chicago Mirror	$1.00	1/1/2001
3	Colleen	Woodburn	2	Chicago Age	$1.50	1/1/2001
3	Colleen	Woodburn	3	Chicago Sun	$2.00	1/5/2001

Table 3.3

Second Normal Form

A relational table is in second normal form if it is in first normal form and all non key attributes are functionally dependent on the entire key. Each attribute in the entity must depend on the entire key, not just part of it. If we draw the dependency diagram for table 3.3, we would get figure 3.2

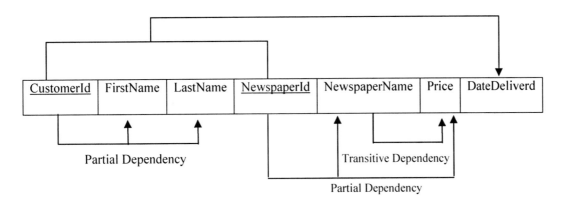

Figure 3.2

By examining figure 3.2, you would notice that the primary key is a composite key composed of CustomerId and NewspaperId. Following the arrows, you would also notice that there are two cases of partial dependency. FirstName and LastName are partially dependent on CustomerId. On the other hand NewspaperName and Price are partially dependent on NewspaperId. Second normal form does not allow partial dependency on primary key. To convert this design to second normal form, the original table is decomposed into new tables that satisfy the conditions of the second normal form. We start with the following

- Write each component key on a separate line. Then write the original composite key on the last line.

  CustomerId
  NewspaperId
  CustomerId, NewspaperId

  As there are two component keys and a composite key, the original table is divided into three tables. Let us call these tables as Customer, Newspaper and Delivery. Each component key becomes a primary key in a table.

- Write the dependent attributes after each key. The dependencies for the original keys can be found by examining the arrow in the dependency diagram in figure 3.2. Now the three new tables would become as

  Customer(<u>CustomerId</u>, FirstName, LastName)
  Newspaper(<u>NewspaperId</u>, NewspaperName, Price)
  Delivery(<u>CustomerId</u>, <u>NewspaperId</u>, DateDelivered)

The new dependency diagram for these three tables would look as shown in figure 3.3. As you can see that both partial dependencies has been eliminated and the tables are in second normal form.

Table: Customer

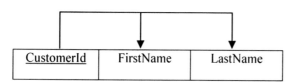

Table: Newspaper

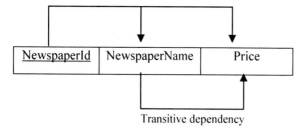

Table: Delivery

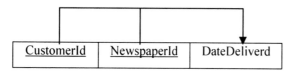

Figure 3.3

Third Normal Form

A relational table is in third normal form if it is in second normal form and any non-key fields does not depend on other non-key fields. In other words the table does not contain any transitive dependencies.

Consider the Newspaper table in figure 3.3. NewspaperId is the primary key, so all of the remaining attributes are functionally dependent on this attribute. However, there is a transitive dependency between Price and NewspaperName. This kind of transitive dependency is not allowed in third normal form and can be eliminated by storing the information in a separate table. Let us call this new table as NewspaperPrice. The primary key for this new table is NewspaperName and it would also include Price as a non key attribute. The original table (Newspaper) would lose the Price attribute but it would retain NewspaperName attribute as a foreign key in order to establish a link between the original table and the newly created table. The new tables should look as following

Customer(CustomerId, FirstName, LastName)

Newspaper(NewspaperId, NewspaperName)

NewspaperPrice(NewspaperName, Price)

Delivery(CustomerId, NewspaperId, DateDelivered)

Now all the tables are in third normal form as we eliminated the transitive dependency. In real world most of the tables would have more attributes then they are shown here. Just for the sake of simplicity the minimum attributes has been shown in these tables. In a normalized database, redundancy is reduced, and this in effect reduces storage requirements. Each entity is represented only one time, thereby increasing data integrity because you only have to look for data in one place. Query performance is increased by creating more compact rows of data. It becomes easier and faster to locate and retrieve multiple record queries.

Integrity Rules

Integrity rules are designed to keep your data consistent, correct and compliant with your business rules. The main reason to use databases rather than spreadsheets to store data is that databases are designed to use integrity rules to help prevent unwanted data into the database in the first place. The four types of data integrity rules are

- Entity integrity
- Domain integrity
- Referential integrity
- User defined integrity

Entity Integrity

The one basic requirement that your data must fulfill to ensure entity integrity is that every row must be unique. No two rows can contain the same data. Each entity needs to have a primary key, which consists of a unique characteristic or set of characteristics that distinguish it from other entities of the same type. Primary keys consist of a column or columns that contain unique values, so that no row of data is ever exactly the same as another row of data. For every instance of an entity, the value of the primary key must exist, must be unique and can not be null.

Domain Integrity

Domain integrity enforces restrictions on the values you can enter in any column, enforcing business rules particular to your application. Domain integrity is used to enforce a range (domain) of values by restricting the type (through data types), the format (through CHECK constraints and rules in MS SQL) or the range of possible values (through foreign key constraints, CHECK constraints, and rules in MS SQL). For example, you won't be able to enter text in a domain that is defined as a date. The more you do to keep bad data from being entered, the less you need to worry about handling bad data later.

Referential Integrity

Referential integrity requires that every foreign key value match a primary key value in an associated table. Referential integrity ensures that you can correctly and fully navigate between related entities. Without referential integrity, it is possible to have data in child entities that has no corresponding data in the parent entity. This type of data is referred to as orphaned. Without proper referential integrity, it is possible to create orphaned records when you insert, update or delete data in a table. MS Access uses foreign key constraints to maintain referential integrity. In MS SQL, referential integrity is maintained through foreign key constraints, CHECK constraints, Triggers and stored procedures.

User Defined integrity

User defined integrity encompasses all other business rules that don't fit into entity, domain and referential integrity concepts. For example, in a medical database the cautions field of the prescription table should include "Do not drive while using this medication". Such a rule can not be expressed through the three defined integrity rules. Business rules in MS SQL are commonly implemented using triggers, rules, or stored procedures.

Chapter 4

Case Study

ABC Computers is a small privately run business. Mr. Brown is the owner of the business. ABC Computers has been in the business of selling computer parts for the last ten years. Currently, Mr. Brown has four employees. Last year, Mr. Brown on his trip to China, found a new supplier who could provide computer parts for much lower price than the local suppliers. Eighty per cent of Mr. Brown's parts could be provided by the newly found Chinese supplier. The other twenty percent parts are supplied by local suppliers. As Mr. Brown is getting a low price from overseas, he can pass on these lower prices to the end customers. This made the business grow ten fold. To deal with this increase in business, Mr. Brown has to hire more employees. He is thinking of hiring ten more employees. He is also thinking of having some kind of database for his order entry system. At the moment, he does not have any database for his business. Things are done the old fashioned way. In the past, Mr. Brown's priority has been to keep all the expenses as low as possible. Therefore, things were kept as simple as possible. Currently customers are given a hand written invoice after a purchase. A carbon copy of the invoice is left in the invoice book for the accountant and warranty purposes. These invoice books are labeled by the month of the year. At the start of the month, a new invoice book is started. If a customer brings a defective part which is under warranty, the employee compares the customer's invoice with the invoice in the book for that date. If both match, the customer is given a new or a refurbished part. The faulty part is sent to the supplier in the next batch.

With the increase in business, keeping this kind of system has become very difficult. Mr. Brown is thinking of developing some kind of database that could do the existing functions and some additional functions. You are a database developer and have been asked to develop a database for his business. You started working on developing a database for Mr. Brown in the following manner.

Analysis

The analysis phase is to find out about the current system and what are the requirements of the new system. During the analysis we will find out the following

- Define a mission statement for the database
- Identify mission objectives
- Identify users requirements
- Identify system requirements

We will use the following techniques to do the analysis

- Observing the business in operation
- Examining the documentation

- Interviewing

Observing business in operation

If you have a first hand experience of the task that you want to computerize, you are most likely to understand the problems associated with it. One of the most effective ways of understanding the current system is to observe the business. During the observation, you want to know as much as possible about the activity. You can participate in an activity or watch a person performing the activity. This technique is also very helpful when the validity of data collected through other techniques is in question.

You call Mr. Brown and tell him that you would like to observe the business first hand. You both schedule a meeting for 11:00 AM. At 11:00 you show up at ABC Computers.

A <u>customer</u> walks in and looks around in the shop. A few minutes later a <u>salesman</u> comes to him.

Salesman: Do you need any help?

Customer: I am looking for a <u>DVD burner</u>.

The Salesman takes him to where the DVD burners are and shows him different DVD burners.

Customer: Why the prices vary so much?

Salesman: Each DVD burner has its own software. The more expensive ones can do rewriting and creating labels for your DVDs.

Customer: Ok, I will take this one.

The salesman takes him to the counter where the invoices are issued.

Salesman: <u>How do you want to pay</u>?

Customer: Cash.

Salesman: What is your name?

Customer: Jim Francis.

Salesman: May I have your phone number?

Customer: Certainly, 905-235-1234. Looking around, do you guys sell laptops?

Salesman: Yes, we do.

Customer: I might get one for Christmas.

Salesman: I can offer you a very good price on a laptop. This DVD burner comes with one year warranty. If it breaks down in first ten days, we will replace it for you. After that, we have to send it to the <u>supplier</u>.

Salesman: Finishes writing the <u>invoice</u>. A carbon copy of the invoice is left in the invoice book.

The salesman gives him an invoice and says him good bye.

After ten minutes another customer walks in with something in his hand.

Salesman: What can I do for you?

Customer: I bought a <u>hard drive</u> five months ago and now it is dead.

Salesman: Do you have an <u>invoice</u> with you?

Customer: Yes I do. He hands him his invoice.

Salesman: Goes to where old invoices are kept. Takes out the invoice book for that month and compares customer's invoice with the copy in the invoice book. Both match. Ok, I will go upstairs and check a refurbished hard disk of the same size. If I find it, I will give you the refurbished one otherwise I have to send it to the supplier.

Customer: That is fine with me.

Salesman: Goes upstairs and finds one refurbished hard drive. You were lucky, I found one. Otherwise you have to wait for two weeks to get a part from a supplier.

Customer: Thanks very much.

Salesman: He gives the customer his invoice and the hard drive. Bye.

A few minutes later, the phone rings and the salesman pick up the phone.

Salesman: ABC Computers, Carl speaking.

Customer: Good morning! I am looking for a 17" Samsung monitor. Do you have one in stock?

Salesman: Yes we do.

Customer: What is the price?

Salesman: $500.

Customer: I will come in an hour and pick it up.

Salesman: Sure, Bye.

Customer: Bye.

After an hour the customer shows up.

Customer: I called a while ago to pick up a 17" Samsung monitor.

Salesman: Oh yes, you spoke to me. The salesman picks up the trolley and brings the monitor. Here is your monitor.

Customer: Ok, thanks. The customer looks at the monitor.

Salesman: How do you want to pay?

Customer: Do you accept visa?

Salesman: Yes we do.

Customer: Gives his visa card to the salesman.

Salesman: Manually processes the credit card and asks the customer for his signature.

Customer: Signs the credit card receipt.

Salesman: Makes an invoice and hands it over to the customer. Where is your car?

Customer: In front of the store.

Salesman: Ok, I will give you a hand and load it into your car.

Customer: Thanks.

Salesman: Loads the monitor into his car. Bye.

Customer: Thanks very much. Bye.

So far by looking at the business, we identified the following entities.

- Customer
- Employee (salesman)
- Product (DVD burner, Hard disk and so on)
- Invoice
- Supplier
- PaymentMethod (How do you want to pay?)

Examining business documentation

Going through documents, forms and reports related to the current system is a good and quick way of getting insight into the business. Examining business documentation also helps in understanding the problems associated with the current system. If you can clearly explain the current documentation, this means that you have a very good understanding of the current business environment.

While you were at ABC Computers, you thought it would be a good idea to see the current documentation for the business.

You: What kind of documentation do you keep for the business?

Mr. Brown: Not much. The only type of documentation I keep is the invoice book and an excel spreadsheet to keep track of the products I have in stock. This is the reason why I need a database.

You: Can I have a copy of the invoice and the inventory spreadsheet.

Mr. Brown: Certainly. He gives you a copy of the spreadsheet and invoice.

You: Thanks Mr. Brown for your time. Now I have to go. I will contact you or your staff in case I need any further information.

You closely study the documentation in your office. In the inventory spreadsheet, you find product name, manufacturer name, supplier name, quantity in stock, buying price and selling price. On the invoice you find business name (ABC Computers), address and phone number. Invoice number and invoice date. Customer name, address and phone number. Product name, manufacturer name, price, quantity ordered and the total amount paid. Employee making the sale name and payment method. After studying the documentation, you conclude the following entities

- Product
- Supplier
- Invoice
- Customer
- Employee
- PaymentMethod

Interviewing

Interviewing is one of the most important methods of investigation. The purpose of an interview could be finding a fact, verifying a fact, clarifying a fact, identifying requirements and gathering ideas. Interviewing requires good communication skills. Make the interviewee feel a part of the project. Let the interviewee respond to the questions freely and openly.

We will use interviewing as our main toll to

- Define a mission statement for the database
- Identify mission objectives
- Identify users requirements
- Identify systems requirements

Define a mission statement for the database

A mission statement defines the main purpose of a database application. A mission statement should be general and should not describe specific tasks. A person who is driving the project is the person who is going to define the mission statement. In our case, it is the owner who is behind the project. You schedule an interview with Mr. Brown. You start asking him the following questions.

You: What is the purpose of your company?
Owner: We sell computer parts. Recently we started selling laptops too.
You: Why do you think you need a database?
Owner: In the past our manual system worked fine as we did not have many customers. Now as the number of customers has increased, it is very difficult to carry on the present system. I need to computerize the whole process which will result in productivity and efficiency.
You: How do you think that a database will solve your problems?
Owner:
- The database will allow orders to be entered into the system as they are received from customers
- Track inventory levels of each product as the products are sold
- Generate customer invoices
- Identify the best customers so that letters can be sent out inviting them to sale and special events

Responses to these questions should help in defining a mission statement for this database. You concluded the following mission statement.

"The purpose of ABC Computers database is to computerize the current system, to maintain the data that computer parts business generate and to provide a customer service"

Identify mission objectives

Once you define the mission statement, the next step is to identify the mission objectives. Each mission objective should identify a particular task that the database must support. Each objective should define a single general task which is free from excess detail. To get a complete range of mission objectives, you should interview the staff in different roles. We will interview each one of them. Remember sometimes you may not get the perfect answers to your questions. If you are in doubt, revisit the questions. Building a database is as much of an art as a science.

When you ask a question from a user, you have to derive objectives from the statements. Some of the objectives are directly stated with in the response and are explicit. Some of the objectives are not directly stated in the response and are implicit. As a database developer, you would make some assumptions based on your past experience to find these hidden (implicit) objectives within a statement. Consider the following example
You: What kind of tasks do you do during a typical day?

Tom: I answer questions about different products and its availability. I restock the shelves and file up the paper work. I also update the inventory spreadsheet as products are sold and new products arrive.

The answer explicitly states the need to maintain information on product. You can also find two pieces of implicit information within the statement. Tom is answering questions about products. You can make the assumption that the person doing the query about a product is a customer. Tom also answers questions about the availability of a product. You can make an assumption that Tom must be dealing with suppliers too in order to answer questions about the availability of a product. So we found one explicit and two implicit mission objectives within Tom's statement and they are

- To maintain data on products
- To maintain data on customers
- To maintain data on suppliers

There are three types of people working at ABC Computers, the owner, a senior salesman and the salespeople. Here is your interview with the owner.

You: What is your job description?
Owner: I am the owner and make sure the smooth running of the business.
You: What kind of tasks do you do during a typical day?
Owner: I monitor the business overall including customer's orders. I do hiring of employees and buying of products from suppliers.
You: What kind of data do you work with?
Owner: I work with data about employees, products, customers, suppliers and orders.
You: What kind of reports do you work with?
Owner: Currently we can not generate any kind of reports. I would like to have reports on products and customers.
You: What kind of things do you keep track of?
Owner: I almost track every thing related to the business including employees, products, customers, suppliers and customer's orders.
You: What kind of service does your company provide to your customers?
Owner: My business provides the best customer service and the most competitive price for computer parts in the market.

Now we will ask the same questions from Alex who is a senior salesman

You: What is your job description?
Senior Salesman: I am a senior salesman. I supervise all sales employees. In the absence of the owner, I have the authority to make decisions.
You: What kind of tasks do you do during a typical day?
Senior Salesman: I assign employees specific duties such as dealing with customers, restocking shelves, filing up paper work such as invoices from suppliers and updating the stock inventory in excel spreadsheet. I also answer queries about any product.
You: What kind of data do you work with?

Senior Salesman: I work with data about employees, products, customers, orders and suppliers.

You: What kind of reports do you work with?

Senior Salesman: Currently we can not generate any reports as we do not have any kind of database. It would be nice to have reports on products in stock and print invoices.

You: What kind of things do you keep track of?

Senior Salesman: I make sure that enough staff is on duty, enough products are in store and customer's orders are filled up on time.

You: What kind of service does your company provide to your customers?

Senior Salesman: We try to provide the best customer service in the computer parts market. We want the customer to have a good experience by dealing with us.

You will ask the same questions from a salesman

You: What is your job description?

Salesman: I am a salesman and I deal directly with customers.

You: What kind of tasks do you do during a typical day?

Salesman: I answer questions from customers about different products. I process orders, write invoices, restock the shelves and file up the paperwork. I also update the inventory spreadsheet as products are sold and new products arrive.

You: What kind of data do you work with?

Salesman: I work with data about customers, products, orders, suppliers and invoices.

You: What kind of reports do you work with?

Salesman: none

You: What kind of things do you keep track of?

Salesman: I keep track of whether certain products are in stock and orders are processed on time.

You: What kind of service your company provides to your customers?

Salesman: We provide customer service to our customers. We answer queries about products in stock. Normally a customer would ask about the specifications of a product and whether that product suits their needs.

Interviewing every person involved in the business helped us in identifying the mission objectives. From these interviews we conclude the following mission objectives.

To maintain (enter, update and delete) data on employees
To maintain (enter, update and delete) data on customers
To maintain (enter, update and delete) data on products
To maintain (enter, update and delete) data on suppliers
To maintain (enter, update and delete) data on customer's orders
To track the status of products in stock
To track the status of customer's orders
To print invoices
To report on product in stock
To report on customers orders

Mission objectives should give you some idea what kind of entities should you include in your ER diagram. Mission objectives could also help in finding out what kind of form should you build into your database. So far from these objectives we conclude the following entities.

- Employee
- Customer
- Product
- Supplier
- Order
- Invoice

Identify user's requirements

User requirements describe in detail the data kept in the database and how to use it. In other words it helps in identifying the attributes related to the entities. During the analysis phase we used the following methods

- Observing the business in operation
- Examining the documentation
- Interviewing (Identifying mission objectives)

By combining the resulting entities from each method, we ended up in the following entities

- Employee
- Customer
- Product
- Supplier
- Invoice
- Order
- PaymentMethod

Now the next step is to find more detail about each one of these entities. The answer to your first question will give you the possible attributes for each entity. The answer to your second question will give you an idea of what kind of form do you need for the end user to enter or edit data. You can use any of the previously discussed techniques to find more detail about each entity. We will use interviewing our main tool. We start asking the following questions from the owner.

You: What kind of information needs to be held about each Employee?
Owner: I keep an employee name, phone number and address.

The owner gave you some explicit information about an employee's attributes. You also have to find the implicit information (implicit attributes) from the statement about an employee. As an experienced database developer, you know that each employee should be given an employee number which is unique through out the company. An employee name is made up of first name and last name. An address is composed of street address, city, region (state or province) and postal code. We ended up in the following attributes

Possible attributes: EmployeeId, EmpLName, EmpFName, EmpAddress, EmpCity, EmpRegion, EmpPostalCode, EmpPhoneNo,

You: What kind of things do you do with the information on an Employee?
Owner: I need to enter details about each new employee and delete it when they leave. I also need an employee's name on each invoice. The main purpose of this exercise is to track down who made the sale. At the end of year, employees are paid bonuses according to their performance.

Possible form: To maintain (enter, update and delete) data on employees.

You: What kind of information needs to be held about each Customer?
Owner: We keep a customer's name, phone number and address.

Possible attributes: CustomerId, CustLName, CustFName, CustAddress, CustCity, CustRegion, CustPostalCode, CustPhoneNo

You: What kind of things do you do with the information on a Customer?
Owner: We need to enter details about each new customer. This information is used for warranty purposes. We should also be able to change the information for an existing customer. I also need to list the names of the customers who are the most valuable.

Possible form: To maintain (enter, update and delete) data on customers.

You: What kind of information needs to be held about each Product?
Owner: We need to keep a product name, manufacturer name, quantity in stock and selling price.

Possible attributes: ProductId, ProdName, Make (manufacturer name), QtyInStock, Price

You: What kind of things do you do with the information on a Product?
Owner: We need to enter details about each new product. We need to know how many products are in stock and what is the selling price?

Possible form: To maintain (enter, update and delete) data on a product.

You: What type of information needs to be held about each Supplier?
Owner: Supplier name, phone number and address.

Possible attributes: SupplierId, SuppName, SuppAddress, SuppCity, SuppRegion, SuppPostalCode, SuppPhoneNo

You: What kind of things do you do with the information on a Supplier?

Owner: I need to enter details about a supplier. Some time if a customer enquires about the availability of a new product or a sold out product, one of my employees may call the supplier about the availability of that product.

Possible form: To maintain (enter, update and delete) data on a supplier.

You: What kind of information needs to be held about each Order?

Owner: Order number and order date. The order number should be unique for each order.

Possible attributes: OrderId, OrderDate

You: What kind of things do you do with the information on an Order?

Owner: We need to enter details about each order. In order to process an order, we need to know customer's information, product being ordered details, employee who took the order and method of payment information.

Possible form: To maintain (enter, update and delete) data on an order.

You: What kind of information needs to be held about each Invoice?

Owner: An Invoice should have an invoice number and order date when it is printed. This information is crucial for warranty purposes. All the order information should be on the invoice. Currently the invoice number on each page in the invoice book acts as an invoice number. The rest of the order information is hand written to the invoice page.

Possible attributes: InvoiceId.

You: What kind of things do you do with the information on an Invoice?

Owner: We print an invoice with all the order information.

Possible form: No data entry form is required. Invoice printing capability is required.

You: What kind of information needs to be held about PaymentMethod?

Owner: PaymentMethod can include Cash, Credit card and Debit card information. This information should be on each invoice. This way we would know how each invoice was paid.

Possible attribute: PymntMethodId, PaymentMethod

You: What kind of things do you do with the information on PaymentMethod?

Owner: I need the payment method information on each invoice to show how each invoice was paid off.

Possible form: No data entry form is required. PaymentMethod information is only required on an invoice.

We asked all the questions from the owner. As ABC Computers is a small company and the owner can answer most of your questions about the company. In case of a bigger and complex company you have to ask these questions different individuals in their positions to get you the right answers. This is your job as a database developer to ask the right questions from the right people. This will help you in producing a good quality entity relationship diagram. We will have an in depth look into entity relationship in topics ahead.

Identifying system requirements

The next step in the analysis phase is to find out system requirements of the database that we are designing. Again we will use interviewing as a way of finding this information from the owner.

You: Is any of the data confidential?
Owner: I would like to have the database password protected.
You: How long do you want to keep data?
Owner: I would like to keep data on customers for 3 years so that we know our customer's interests and we can mail them flyers on special offers. We also need this data for accounting purposes.
You: What kind of protection from failure do you want for your database?
Owner: I need a backup of the database during non business hours.

By asking similar questions, you can find out more about systems requirements.

Identifying entities

In the previous chapters we discussed relational database theory. A clear understanding of that theory is necessary and we are going to build on that theory. So far by observing the business, examining the documentation and interviewing the users we came up with the following possible entities

- Employee
- Customer
- Product
- Supplier
- Order
- Invoice
- PaymentMethod

Remember that all the decisions you make about the entities become your business rules. Let us create a separate rectangle for each entity identified in ABC Computers database.

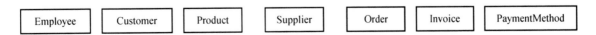

Figure 4.1 Entities identified in ABC database

Identifying the relationship between entities

After you choose your database entities, you need to consider the relationship between them. Remember that we are looking for direct relationship only. Relationships are not always obvious, but all the ones worth recording must be found. The only way to ensure that all the relationships are found is to list all possible relationships exhaustively.

A convenient way to discover the relationship is to prepare a matrix that names all the entities on the rows and again on the columns as shown in figure 4.2. Let us first consider the diagonal cells to find the recursive relationships. We start asking the following questions

Q: Can a single Employee be associated with one or more employees?
Answer: There are two kinds of employees, Salesman and a Senior Salesman. There could be a recursive relationship between employees as one employee manages other employee. This kind of situation depends on the business requirements. To find out whether you should resolve this recursive relationship or not, you should check with the owner. You pick up the phone and call Mr. Brown.
You: Hello Mr. Brown!
Owner: Hello! What can I do for you?
You: You have two kinds of employees, salesman and senior salesman. Is the type of data required for the senior salesman different from what is required for an ordinary salesman?
Owner: No, I consider both the same.
You: Ok, Thank you.
As you found from Mr. Brown that there is no user requirement to resolve this recursive relationship, so this is one of your business rules.
Employee-Employee: No direct relationship exists.

Let us proceed to the rest of the intersecting columns.

Customer-Customer:
Q: Can a single Customer be associated with one or more customers?
Answer: No

	Employee	Customer	Product	Supplier	Order	Invoice	PaymentMethod
Employee	?						
Customer		None					
Product			None				
Supplier				None			
Order					None		
Invoice						None	
PaymentMethod							None

Figure 4.2 A matrix that reflects the entities for ABC Computers

Product-Product:
Q: Can a single Product be associated with one or more products?
Answer: No

Supplier-Supplier

Q: Can a single Supplier be associated with one or more suppliers?

Answer: No

Order-Order:

Q: Can a single Order be associated with one or more orders?

Answer: No

Invoice-Invoice:

Q: Can a single Invoice be associated with one or more invoices?

Answer: No

PaymentMethod-PaymentMethod:

Q: Can a single PaymentMethod be associated with one or more PaymentMethods?

Answer: No

Write "none" in all the diagonal cells as there does not exist any recursive relationship.

Next we will go through each intersecting entities in the matrix one by one to find the relationship between entities. Let us start from the first row.

Employee-Customer: You may think that there is a relationship between an employee and a customer as an employee takes an order from a customers. But this is an indirect relationship and it is through the order entity. We are looking for a direct relationship. Therefore, we can say that there is no direct relationship between Employee and Customer entities.

Employee-Product: No direct relationship exists.

Employee-Supplier: No direct relationship exists.

Employee-Order: One employee can process how many orders?

Answer: One or many. We will write 1-N in the cell as shown in 4.3.

Employee-Invoice: No direct relationship exists.

Employee-PaymentMethod: No direct relationship exists.

Customer-Employee: No direct relationship exists.

Customer-Product: The relationship between Customer and Product is through Order entity. A Customer places an Order. An Order contains Products. Therefore, there is no direct relationship between Customer and Product.

Customer-Supplier: No direct relationship exists.

Customer-Order: One Customer can place how many Orders?

Answer: one or many. Therefore, we will write 1-N in the cell.

Customer-Invoice: No direct relationship exists.

Customer-PaymentMethod: No direct relationship exists.

Product-Employee: No direct relationship exists.

Product-Customer: The relationship between Product and Customer is through Order entity. A Customer places an Order. An Order contains a Product. Therefore, there is no direct relationship between Product and Customer.

Product-Supplier: One Product can be supplied by how many Suppliers?

Answer: Not sure. You call Mr. Brown to check the type of relationship between Product and Supplier.

You: Hello Mr. Brown.

Owner: Hello. What can I do for you?

You: I have a question about the relationship between Product and Supplier. Can the same product be supplied by many suppliers?

Owner: No. Different suppliers can supply the same type of product but of a different brand. For example one supplier can supply Samsung 17 inch monitors and another supplier can supply Hitachi 17 inch monitors. They both are monitors but of a different brand.

You: Thank you Mr. Brown. That is all I wanted to ask. Bye.

Conclusion: One product can be supplied by one supplier. Therefore, we will write 1-1 in the cell.

Product-Order: One product can be included in how many orders?

Answer: One or many. We will write 1-N in the cell.

Product-Invoice: No direct relationship exists.

Product-PaymentMethod: No direct relationship exists.

Supplier-Employee: No direct relationship.

Supplier-Customer: No direct relationship.

Supplier-Product: One supplier can supply how many products?

Answer: One or many. Therefore, we will write 1-N in the cell.

Supplier-Order: No direct relationship.

Supplier-Invoice: No direct relationship.

Supplier-PaymentMethod: No direct relationship.

Order-Employee: One Order can be processed by how many employees?

Answer: One. We will write 1-1 in the cell.

Order-Customer: One order can be placed by how many customers?

Answer: One. We will write 1-1 in the cell.

Order-Product: One order can have how many products?

Answer: One or many. We will write 1-N in the cell.

Order-Supplier: No direct relationship exists.

Order-Invoice: One order can be associated with how many invoices?

Answer: One. We will write 1-1 in the cell.

Order-PaymentMethod: No direct relationship.

Invoice-Employee: No direct relationship.

Invoice-Customer: No direct relationship.

Invoice-Products: No direct relationship.

Invoice-Supplier: No direct relationship exists.

Invoice-Order: One invoice can be associated with how many orders?

Answer: One. We will write 1-1 in the cell.

Invoice-PaymentMethod: One invoice can be paid in how many ways?

Answer: Here we make the assumption that an invoice can be paid through one of the available payment methods (Cash, Credit card or Debit card). An Invoice can not be paid half cash and half credit card. This is our business rule. Therefore, we will write 1-1 in the cell.

PaymentMethod-Employee: No direct relationship exists.
PaymentMethod-Customer: No direct relationship exists.
PaymentMethod-Product: No direct relationship exists.
PaymentMethod-Supplier: No direct relationship exists.
PaymentMethod-Order: No direct relationship exists.
PaymentMethod-Invoice: One PaymentMethod can be associated with how many invoices?
Answer: One. We will write 1-1 in this cell.

Now the new matrix should look as shown in figure 4.3.

	Employee	Customer	Product	Supplier	Order	Invoice	PaymentMethod
Employee	None				1:N		
Customer		None			1:N		
Product			None	1:1	1:N		
Supplier			1:N	None			
Order	1:1	1:1	1:N		None	1:1	
Invoice					1:1	None	1:1
PaymentMethod						1:1	None

Figure 4.3 An updated matrix that reflects the relationship between the entities

Let us look at the following two relationships in the matrix

Employee-Order: 1:N
Order-Employee: 1:1

As you can see, from one side it is 1: N relationship and from the other side it is 1:1. Now how do you determine the final relationship between Employee and Order entities?

There is a formula to calculate the final relationship. Here it is

1:1 + 1:1 = 1:1
1: N + 1:1 = 1: N
1: N + 1: N = M: N

Applying this formula, the final relationships between Employee and Order entities would be

Employee and Order: 1:N + 1:1 = 1:N

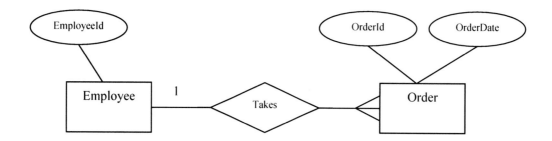

Figure 4.4 shows the final relationship between Employee and Order entities

Applying the same rules to the rest of the relationships would give us the following

Customer-Order: 1:N
Order-Customer: 1:1
Final relationship between Customer and order = 1:N + 1:1 = 1:N

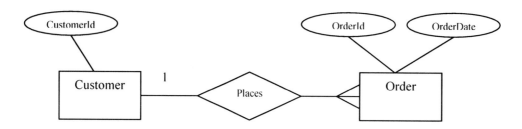

Figure 4.5 shows the final relationship between Customer and Order entities

Product-Supplier: 1:1
Supplier-Product: 1:N
Final relationship between Supplier and Product = 1:1 + 1:N = 1:N

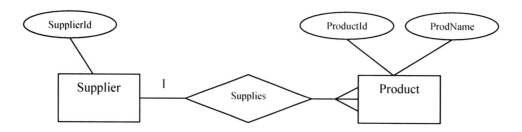

Figure 4.6 shows the final relationship between Supplier and Product entities

Product-Order: 1:N
Order-Product: 1:N
Final relationship between Order and Product = 1:N + 1:N = M:N

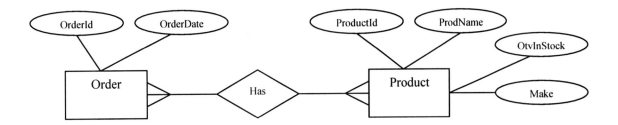

Figure 4.7 shows the final relationship between Order and Product entities

Supplier and Product are already done above
Order and Employee are already done above
Order and Customer are already done above
Order and Product are already done above

Order-Invoice: 1:1
Invoice-Order: 1:1
Final relationship between Order and Invoice = 1:1 + 1:1 = 1:1

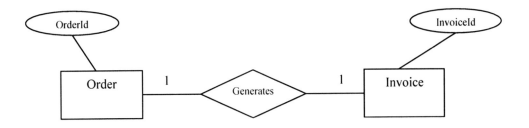

Figure 4.8 shows the final relationship between Order and Invoice entities

Invoice and Order are already done above

Invoice-PaymentMethod: 1:1
PaymentMethod-Invoice: 1:1
Final relationship between Invoice and PaymentMethod = 1:1 + 1:1 = 1:1

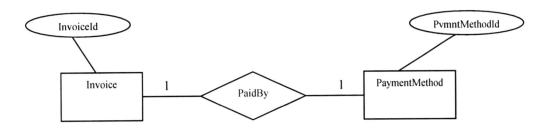

Figure 4.9 shows the final relationship between Invoice and PaymentMethod entities

In figure 4.7, the relationship between Order and Product is M: N (many-to-many). One order has many products and one product can be in many orders. The relational database model does not support many-to-many relationships. The main reason behind not supporting many-to-many relationship is that one or more entities may be hidden in the relationship. Splitting the many-to-many relationship brings those hidden entities. We can convert this relationship into associative entity if two conditions are true. First it should be a many-to-many relationship which is true. Second the relationship should have its own attributes. We can attach the following attribute to the Has relationship

- Quantity: The number of Products ordered by the customer

Now the Has relationship has all the properties of an associative entity. Convert this relationship to an associative entity and call this entity as OrderDetail. Let us call the Quantity attribute as QtyOrdered and attach it to the OrderDetail entity. Figure 4.10 shows this transformation.

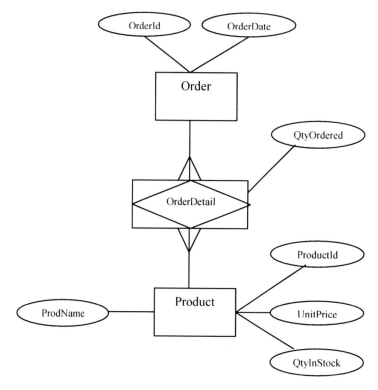

Figure 4.10 ER diagram with the new associative entity

By converting the Has relationship to an associative OrderDetail entity, the crow foot moved from both sides to the associative entity. As OrderDetail is an associative entity, it will have the primary keys from both entities. The combination of these two primary keys can provide a unique key. Therefore, it will become a primary key for OrderDetail entity. To confirm that we did not end up in another many-to-many relationship, let us draw these tables and load some data into it as shown in figure 4.11.

Order

OrderId	OrderDate
O1	2/1/2005
O2	2/2/2005
O3	2/2/2005
O4	2/3/2005

OrderDetail

OrderId	ProductId	QtyOrdered
O1	P1	1
O1	P3	2
O2	P1	1
O2	P2	2
O2	P3	1

Product

ProductId	ProdName	UnitPrice	QtyInStock
P1	100 GB Seagate Hard Disk drive	$50	10
P2	200 GB Seagate Hard Disk drive	$100	15
P3	128 MB IBM RAM	$50	15
P4	17 " Samsung monitor	$300	10
P5	1.44 MB Panasonic Floppy drive	$20	8
P6	Sony DVD writer	$100	20

Figure 4.11

OrderId O1 appears once in Order table as it is the primary key but appears twice in OrderDetail table and consists of products P1 and P3. This is a one-to-many relationship between Order and OrderDetail. ProductId P1 appears once in Product table as it is the primary key but appears twice in OrderDetail table and is a part of order O1 and O2. This is a one-to-many relationship between Product and OrderDetail. Both relationships follow what we see in real life. We can stop here as all hidden entities have been discovered. If the splitting of the original Has relationship had not been performed, the OrderDetail entity and its attributes would have remained hidden.

Now we will draw the final ER diagram for ABC Computers database by combining all the previous ER diagrams as shown in figure 4.12. To save space, some of the attributes related to the entities are not shown in the diagram.

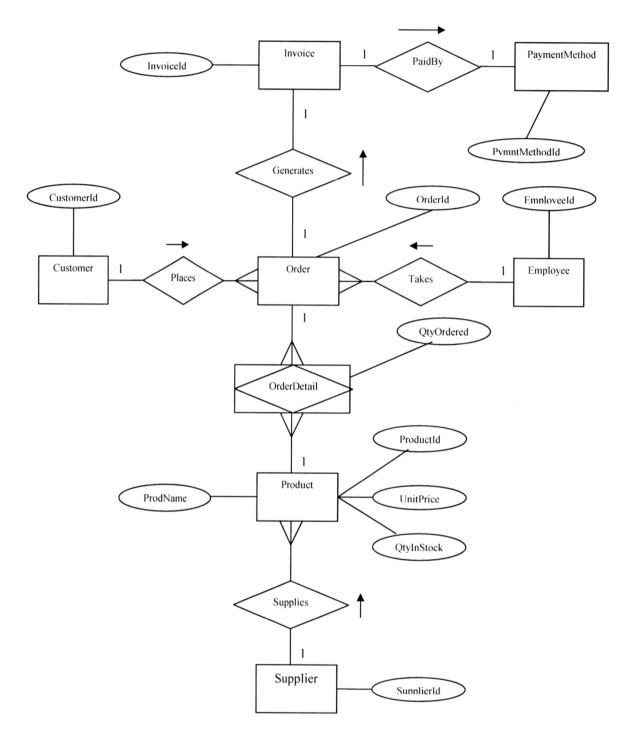

Figure 4.12 Entity relationship diagram for ABC Computers database

Identifying the right attributes for each entity

During the finding of user requirements, the answer to our first question gave us the possible attributes for most of our entities. Then in the previous topic (Identifying the relationship between entities), we found a new associative entity called OrderDetail. The newly found entity got it attributes during the relationship phase. One of the attribute was

QtyOrdered. The other two attributes were the primary keys (OrderId & ProductId) from the two tables (Order & Product). Here is each entity along with its attributes.

Employee entity
Attributes: EmployeeId, EmpLName, EmpFName, EmpAddress, EmpCity, EmpRegion, EmpPostalCode, EmpPhoneNo

Customer entity
Attributes: CustomerId, CustLName, CustFName, CustAddress, CustCity, CustRegion, CustPostalCode, CustPhoneNo

Product entity
Attributes: ProductId, ProdName, Make, QtyInStock, UnitPrice

Supplier entity
Attributes: SupplierId, SuppName, SuppAddress, SuppCity, SuppRegion, SuppPostalCode, SuppPhoneNo

Order entity
Attributes: OrderId, OrderDate

Invoice entity
Attributes: InvoiceId

PaymentMethod entity
Attributes: PymntMethodId, PaymentMethod

OrderDetail entity
Attributes: OrderId, ProductId, QtyOrdered

Choosing the right primary key
The next step is to find the right primary key for each entity in our ER diagram. The relational model dictates that every row in a database must be unique. If the database allows duplicate rows, you will be forever lost. You can guarantee uniqueness for a table by defining a primary key. The primary key for a table is an attribute or a set of attributes that uniquely identifies a specific instance of an entity. Every entity must have a primary key whose value uniquely identifies instances of the entity. This concept is referred to as entity integrity or row integrity.

In a relationship, a primary key is used to refer from one table to specific records in another table. A primary key is called a foreign key when it is referred to from another table. During the user requirements discussion, we found all the possible attributes for our entities. From those attributes we have to choose the attribute that is best suited to be a primary key. They are listed below. Each primary key is underlined to show that it is a primary key. The OrderDetail table is already having a composite primary key composed of a primary key from Order table and Product table.

Employee entity: <u>EmployeeId</u>
Customer entity: <u>CustomerId</u>
Product entity: <u>ProductId</u>
Supplier: <u>SupplierId</u>
Order: <u>OrderId</u>
Invoice: <u>InvoiceId</u>
PaymentMethod: <u>PymntMethodId</u>
OrderDetail: <u>OrderId</u>, <u>ProductId</u>

Data requirements

The next step is what data we are going to hold in each table. In the previous topic we found all possible attributes for each entity. Microsoft Access refers to attributes as fields. As we are implementing this database in Access, we need to be familiar with various data types in Access. Some of the most common ones are the following

Text: Used for storing text up to 255 characters. Commonly used for name, address, telephone number etc. Phone numbers are more properly stored in a text because they may have spaces, dashes and even brackets.

Number: Used to store numeric data. Access allows you to choose byte (can store numbers between 0-255), integer (for whole numbers between -32,768 and 32,767), long integer (is the default and used for large whole numbers) etc

AutoNumber: This data type generates a series of numbers automatically incremented by one. Commonly used for a primary key.

Currency: Used for holding currency amounts.

Boolean: Used to hold Yes/No or True/False

Date/Time   Used to hold date / or time

Memo: Used to hold additional notes or background information. Notes could be up to 64,000 characters.

Now for each entity in figure 4.12, we will create a table as shown in figure 4.13 that includes the attributes that we found during the user requirements phase. For final attributes, refer to topic identifying the right attributes for each entity.

Employee

Attribute	Data type	Description
<u>EmployeeId</u>	AutoNumber	Primary key, increments automatically
EmpLName	Text	
EmpFName	Text	
EmpAddress	Text	Street address
EmpCity	Text	
EmpRegion	Text	State or province
EmpPostalCode	Text	
EmpPhoneNo	Text	

Customer

Attribute	Data type	Description
CustomerId	AutoNumber	Primary key, increments automatically
CustLName	Text	
CustFName	Text	
CustAddress	Text	Street address
CustCity	Text	
CustRegion	Text	State or province
CustPostalCode	Text	
CustPhoneNo	Text	

Product

Attribute	Data type	Description
ProductId	AutoNumber	Primary key, increments automatically
ProdName	Text	
Make	Text	Manufacturer name
QtyInStock	Number	
Price	Currency	

Supplier

Attribute	Data type	Description
SupplierId	AutoNumber	Primary key, increments automatically
SupplierName	Text	
SuppAddress	Text	
SuppCity	Text	
SuppRegion	Text	
SuppPostalCode	Text	
SuppPhoneNo	Text	

Order

Attribute	Data type	Description
OrderId	AutoNumber	Primary key, increments automatically
OrderDate	Date/time	

Invoice

Attribute	Data type	Description
InvoiceId	AutoNumber	Primary key, increments automatically

PaymentMethod

Attribute	Data type	Description
PymntMethodId	AutoNumber	Primary key, increments automatically
PaymentMethod	Text	

OrderDetail

Attribute	Data type	Description
OrderId	Number	Foreign key, same as OrderId in Order table, Part of a composite primary key
ProductId	Number	Foreign key, same as ProductId in Product table, Part of a composite primary key
QtyOrdered	Number	

Figure 4.13 Tables developed from ER diagram for ABC Computers database in figure 4.12

Creating relationship between tables

So far most of the tables that we have created for our entities do not show the relationship between the tables. Table OrderDetail is an exception which is an associative entity and shows its relationship to Order table and Product table. To create tables with relationship, we have to revisit the ER diagram in figure 4.12.

Customer-Order relationship: The Customer entity is associated with Order entity through Places relationship. The cardinality between the two is 1:M. Now we will include the primary key attribute of the table on the one side of the relationship as a foreign key in the table that is on the many side of the relationship. Remember that the primary key migrates to the many side. This means that the Customer table will still remain the same but the Order table will get the primary key from the Customer table as a foreign key as shown in figure 4.14.

Employee-Order relationship: The Employee entity is associated with Order entity through Takes relationship. The cardinality between the two is 1:M. Now we will include the primary key attribute of the table on the one side of the relationship as a foreign key in the table that is on the many side of the relationship. This means that the Employee table will still be the same but the Order table will get the primary key from Employee table as a foreign key as shown in figure 4.14.

Order-OrderDetail relationship: The cardinality between the two entities is 1:M. This means that we have to include the primary key attribute from the table on the one side of the relationship as foreign key in the table on the many side of the relationship. The OrderDetail table is already having the primary key from the Order table because of being an associative entity. Therefore, we do not have to worry about this one.

Order-Invoice relationship: The Order entity is associated with Invoice entity through Generates relationship. The cardinality between the two is 1:1. In this case we can include the primary key attribute of one of the table as a foreign key in the other table. Generally you should include the primary key from the mandatory side as a foreign key in the optional side. We take the primary key from Order table and include it in the Invoice table as a foreign key as shown in figure 4.14.

PaymentMethod-Invoice relationship: Here again we are having a cardinality of 1:1 between the two entities. We chose the primary key from PaymentMethod table and include it as a foreign key in the Invoice table as shown in figure 4.14.

Product-OrderDetail relationship: The cardinality between the two entities is 1:M. This implies that we have to include the primary key attribute from the table on the one side of the relationship as foreign key in the table on the many side of the relationship. The OrderDetail table is already having the primary key from the Product table because of being an associative entity. Therefore, we do not have to worry about this one.

Supplier-Product relationship: The cardinality between the two entities is 1:M. We have to include the primary key from the Supplier table as a foreign key in the Product table as shown in figure 4.14.

After all this discussion, we draw the new tables with the new foreign keys. Figure 4.14 shows the new tables.

Employee

Attribute	Data type	Description
EmployeeId	AutoNumber	Primary key, increments automatically
EmpLName	Text	
EmpFName	Text	
EmpAddress	Text	Street address
EmpCity	Text	
EmpRegion	Text	State or province
EmpPostalCode	Text	
EmpPhoneNo	Text	

Customer

Attribute	Data type	Description
CustomerId	AutoNumber	Primary key, increments automatically
CustLName	Text	
CustFName	Text	
CustAddress	Text	Street address
CustCity	Text	
CustRegion	Text	State or province
CustPostalCode	Text	
CustPhoneNo	Text	

Product

Attribute	Data type	Description
ProductId	AutoNumber	Primary key, increments automatically
SupplierId	Number	Foreign key, same as SupplierId in Supplier table
ProdName	Text	
Make	Text	
QtyInStock	Number	
Price	Currency	

Supplier

Attribute	Data type	Description
SupplierId	AutoNumber	Primary key, increments automatically
SupplierName	Text	
SuppAddress	Text	
SuppCity	Text	
SuppRegion	Text	
SuppPostalCode	Text	
SuppPhoneNo	Text	

Order

Attribute	Data type	Description
OrderId	AutoNumber	Primary key, increments automatically
CustomerId	Number	Foreign key, same as CustomerId in Customer table
EmployeeId	Number	Foreign key, same as EmployeeId in Employee table
OrderDate	Date/time	

Invoice

Attribute	Data type	Description
InvoiceId	AutoNumber	Primary key, increments automatically
OrderId	Number	Foreign Key, same as OrderId in Order table
PymntMethodId	Number	Foreign key, same as PymntMethodId in PaymentMethod table

PaymentMethod

Attribute	Data type	Description
PymntMethodId	AutoNumber	Primary key, increments automatically
PaymentMethod	Text	

OrderDetail

Attribute	Data type	Description
OrderId	Number	Foreign key, same as OrderId in Order table, Part of a composite primary key
ProductId	Number	Foreign key, same as ProductId in Product table, Part of a composite primary key
QtyOrdered	Number	

Figure 4.14

Normalizing the tables

Normalization is a process to design a database to achieve the best performance. We will only apply the first three normal forms to our tables as they are the most important.

First normal form

A table is in first normal form if it does not contain any repeating attributes. In other words the value in the database tables must be atomic. Consider the following question that we asked the owner while finding the user requirements.

You: What kind of information needs to be held about each Employee?
Owner: I keep an employee name, phone number and address.

We said that an address is composed of street address, city, state or province (region) and postal code. Splitting the address to its atomic components made the table in first normal form.

Consider the EmpPhoneNo attribute. If an employee has more than one phone number and we would like to have it in the database, this would mean that the Employee table is not in first normal form. The attribute has to be decomposed to identify a weak entity named EmpPhoneNo. As we are not interested in storing multiple phone numbers for an Employee, therefore, we would leave the Employee table as is. Going through each table, all the tables in the database are in first normal form.

Second normal form

A table is in second normal form if it is in first normal form and all non key attributes are functionally dependent on the entire key. This normal form violation can occur in entities where the primary key comprises of multiple attributes. The only table that has a composite key is the OrderDetail table and it is already in second normal form.

Third normal form

Any non key fields must not depend on other non key fields. Going through each table, we can not find any non key fields depending on other non key fields. Therefore, all the tables in the database are in third normal form.

Chapter 5

Creating a database in Access

Access is one of the most popular and powerful database applications available. Using Access, you can easily create a relational database that includes data entry forms, reports and queries. In this chapter we will learn how to create a database in Access. For our case study, it is not important what version of Access we use. Any version starting from Access 2000 onward is fine. We chose Access 2002.

Starting Access

Depending on the options you choose when you install Access 2002, the menu path you use to start Access may differ slightly. Here is what we came across.

- Click on the **start button**. The start menu will appear, then select **All Programs**
- Click on **Microsoft Access**
- The Microsoft Access window will open as shown in figure 5.1

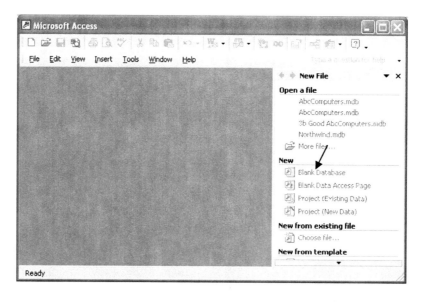

Figure 5.1

Now you have the option of either opening an existing database or creating a new one. We will create a new database from scratch

- Click **Blank database** in the right hand pane. A window as shown in figure 5.2 will open asking you to select a folder and a name for your new database. It is a good idea to create a separate folder for each database.
- Click the arrow to the right of **Save In** box and select **Local Disk (C:)**
- Click the **Create New Folder** button. A **New folder** window will appear as shown in figure 5.3

- Type **ABC Computers** in the window and Click **Ok**. The ABC Computers folder will be created

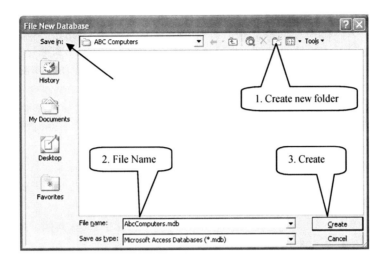

Figure 5.2

Figure 5.3

- In the **File Name** box, type **AbcComputers** and click the **Create** button. Access will automatically add the file extension **.mdb** .This will bring the screen in figure 5.4

Figure 5.4 Main database window

The Database Window

Looking at the title bar of the database window in figure 5.4, you would notice that the default file format is set to Access 2000. A file in Access 2000 file format can be opened in both Access 2000 and Access 2002. A file in Access 2002 format can only be opened in Access 2002. Therefore, we would leave the existing format. The left side of the Access database window includes seven buttons, each corresponding to one of the seven objects that make up an Access database. There are options to open an object, change its design or create a new object. Tables is currently selected. As there are no existing tables to open or design, only the create option is active.

Creating a new table

- In the main database window as shown in figure 5.4, click on **Tables** under **Objects** if not selected
- Click **New** in the Database window toolbar, the new table box will open as shown in figure 5.5

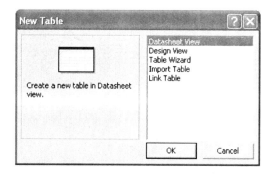

Figure 5.5

- Click **Design View** and click **Ok**. This will bring the screen in figure 5.6

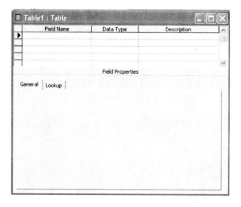

Figure 5.6

Once you are in Table design view, you have to tell Access exactly what fields you want in the table and what type of data should be in each field. Figure 5.7 shows all the tables

89

in figure 4.14. We also added some details into the description to make it easier to understand.

Employee

Attribute	Data type	Description
EmployeeId	AutoNumber	Field size (Long Integer), Indexed: Yes (No Duplicates)
EmpLName	Text	Field size (20), Required: Yes, Indexed: Yes (Duplicates OK)
EmpFName	Text	Field size (20), Required: Yes, Indexed: No
EmpAddress	Text	Field size (50), Required : No, Indexed: No
EmpCity	Text	Field size (20), Required: No, Indexed: No
EmpRegion	Text	Field size (20), Required: No, Indexed: No
EmpPostalCode	Text	Field size (20), Required: No, Indexed: Yes (Duplicates OK)
EmpPhoneNo	Text	Field Size (20), Required: No, Indexed: No

Customer

Attribute	Data type	Description
CustomerId	AutoNumber	Field size (Long Integer), Indexed: Yes (No Duplicates)
CustLName	Text	Field size (20), Required: Yes, Indexed: Yes (Duplicates OK)
CustFName	Text	Field size (20), Required: Yes, Indexed: No
CustAddress	Text	Field size (50), Required : No, Indexed: No
CustCity	Text	Field size (20), Required: No, Indexed: No
CustRegion	Text	Field size (20), Required: No, Indexed: No
CustPostalCode	Text	Field size (20), Required: No, Indexed: Yes (Duplicates OK)
CustPhoneNo	Text	Field Size (20), Required: No, Indexed: No

Product

Attribute	Data type	Description
ProductId	AutoNumber	Field size (Long Integer), Indexed: Yes (No Duplicates)
SupplierId	Number	Field size (Long Integer), Required: No, Indexed: Yes (Duplicates OK)
ProdName	Text	Field Size (50), Required: Yes, Indexed: Yes (Duplicates OK)
Make	Text	Field size (20), Required: Yes, Indexed: No,
QtyInStock	Number	Field size (Integer), Default Value: 0, Required: No, Validation Rule: >= 0, Indexed: No
Price	Currency	Format: Currency, Default Value: 0, Required: No, Indexed: No

Supplier

Attribute	Data type	Description
SupplierId	AutoNumber	Field size (Long Integer), Indexed: Yes (No Duplicates)
SuppName	Text	Field size (20), Required: Yes, Indexed: Yes (Duplicates OK)
SuppAddress	Text	Field size (50), Required : No, Indexed: No
SuppCity	Text	Field size (20), Required: No, Indexed: No
SuppRegion	Text	Field size (20), Required: No, Indexed: No
SuppPostalCode	Text	Field size (20), Required: No, Indexed: Yes (Duplicates OK)
SuppPhoneNo	Text	Field Size (20), Required: No, Indexed: No

Order

Attribute	Data type	Description
OrderId	AutoNumber	Field size (Long Integer), Indexed: Yes (No Duplicates)
CustomerId	Number	Field size (Long Integer), Required: No, Indexed: Yes (Duplicates OK)
EmployeeId	Number	Field size (Long Integer), Required: No, Indexed: Yes (Duplicates OK)
OrderDate	Date/time	Format: Short Date, Default value: Date(), Required : Yes

Invoice

Attribute	Data type	Description
InvoiceId	AutoNumber	Field size (Long Integer), Indexed: Yes (No Duplicates)
OrderId	Number	Field size (Long Integer), Required: No, Indexed: Yes (Duplicates OK)
PymntMethodId	Number	Field size (Long Integer), Required: No, Indexed: Yes (Duplicates OK)

PaymentMethod

Attribute	Data type	Description
PymntMethodId	AutoNumber	Field size (Long Integer), Indexed: Yes (No Duplicates)
PaymentMethod	Text	Field size (10), Required: Yes, Indexed: No

OrderDetail

Attribute	Data type	Description
OrderId	Number	Field size (Long Integer), Required: No, Indexed: Yes (Duplicates OK)
ProductId	Number	Field size (Long Integer), Required: Yes, Indexed: Yes (Duplicates OK)
QtyOrdered	Number	Field Size (Integer), Default Value: 1, Validation Rule: > 0, Required: Yes, Indexed: No

Figure 5.7

- The first table is the Employee table. Enter the first field **EmployeeId** and press tab to move to the **Data Type** field
- Click the Down arrow and select the field type **AutoNumber**
- Tab to the **Description** column and type **Primary key**

You will notice in **Field Properties** in figure 5.8 that the AutoNumber is automatically given a **Field Size** property of **Long Integer**. **New Values** has the property **Increment** which means that this field will increase by 1 for each new employee. The **Indexed** property currently shows **Yes (Duplicates OK)**. Since the EmployeeId is underlined, that means that it is a primary key. We do not want any duplicates for a primary key.

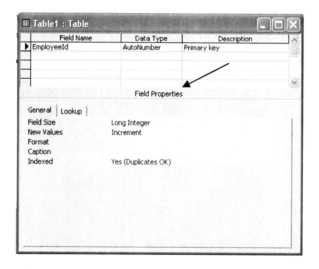

Figure 5.8

- Click on **EmployeeId** field, an arrow will appear in the **Field Selector** column as shown in figure 5.9. Click the **Primary Key** button on the toolbar. A key symbol appears in the field selector next to **EmployeeId**. The **Indexed** property in Field Properties changes to **Yes (No Duplicates)**

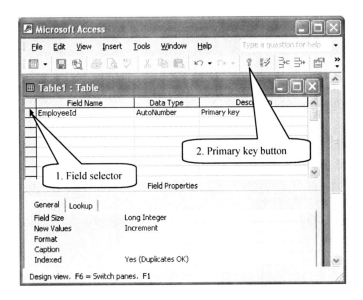

Figure 5.9

- In the next row type **EmpLName**. Tab to the **Data Type** column and the default is **Text**, which is fine. Change the **Field Size** property in the bottom half of the screen from the default 50 characters to 20

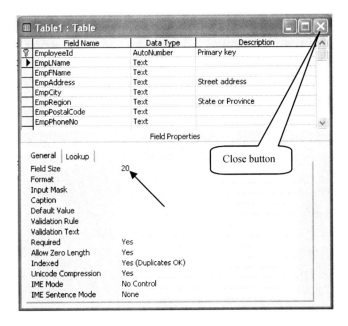

5.10

- Change the **Required** field property from No to Yes (by clicking the down arrow and selecting Yes)
- Change the **Indexed** field property from No to Yes (Duplicates OK) (by clicking the down arrow)
- Leave the rest of the fields properties with default values
- Fill up the rest of the fields (EmpFName, EmpAddress, EmpCity, EmpRegion, EmpPostalCode and EmpPhoneNo) according to the Employee table in figure 5.7

Pay attention to the **Description** column of the **Employee** table in figure 5.7. Once you are finished, your table should look as shown in figure 5.10.

- Click on the **Close button** for the table. A dialog box will open asking if you want to save changes to the design of the table
- Click on **Yes**. The **Save As** dialog box will open. Enter a name of **Employee** in the **Table Name** text box
- Click on **OK**. The main database window will appear. You will see your new table listed now

Create all the tables in Figure 5.7 the same way we created the Employee table. The only exception is OrderDetail table. The procedure to create OrderDetail table is as following.

- In the main database window, click **Tables** if not selected
- Click **New**, Click **Design View** and Click **Ok**. This will bring the screen in figure 5.6
- Enter the first field **OrderId.** Press tab to move to the **Data Type** field

To create a primary key for OrderDetail table, we are joining two **AutoNumber**s to relate the two tables. In this situation, you should select the **Data Type** Number and set the **Field Size** for the Number field to **Long Integer**. If you don't do this, Access will not be able to link the fields.

- Click the down arrow for Data Type and select **Number** if not selected
- Click the down arrow for Field Size and select **Long Integer** if not selected
- Click the down arrow for Indexed and select **Yes(Duplicates OK)** if not selected
- Click in the **Description** column for OrderId and type **Part of a Composite Primary key (Same as OrderId in Order table)**
- Enter the second field **ProductId.** Press tab to move to the **Data Type** field
- Click the down arrow for Data Type and select **Number**
- Click the down arrow for Field Size and select **Long Integer** if not selected
- Click the down arrow for Required and select **Yes**
- Click the down arrow for Indexed and select **Yes(Duplicates OK)** if not selected

- Click in the Description column for ProductId and type **Part of a Composite Primary key (Same as ProductId in Product table)**
- To create a primary key for OrderDetail table, click the field selector for **OrderId** field first, hold down the **Ctrl** key, click the field selector for **ProductId** field and then click the **Primary key** button. A key symbol will appear in the field selector next to **OrderId** and **PrductId**. Now you have created a composite key for OrderDetail table.
- Enter the third field **QtyOrdered.** Press tab to move to the **Data Type** field
- Click the down arrow for **Data Type** and select **Number**
- Click the down arrow for **Field Size** and select **Integer**
- Click in the **Default Value** box and type **1**
- Click the **Validation Rule** box and type **> 0**
- Click the down arrow for **Required** and select **Yes**
- Click on the **Close button** for the table. A dialog box will open asking if you want to save changes to the design of the table
- Click on **Yes**. The **Save As** dialog box will open. Enter **OrderDetail** in the **Table Name** text box
- Click **OK**. The main database window will appear. You will see your new table listed in the window.

Defining the relationship between the tables

The next step after creating tables is to define the relationship between the tables. You can define the relationship by doing the following

- On the main toolbar, Click **Tools, Relationships**

Figure 5.11

- The **Show Table** window will appear as shown in figure 5.12

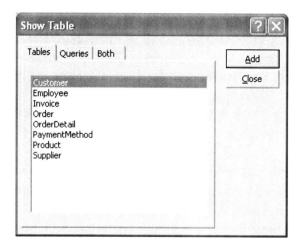

Figure 5.12

- Highlight each table in turn and click **Add**. We want all the tables that we created to appear in the **relationship** window
- Click **Close**

All the tables should be in the **Relationships** window as shown in figure 5.13

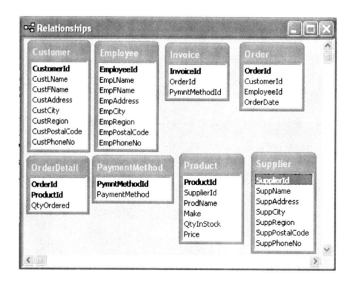

Figure 5.13

Go to Figure 5.7 and look for the tables with the foreign keys. The first table with foreign key is the Product table. The Product table has a foreign key SupplierId from Supplier table. The relationship between the two tables is one-to-many.

- To set the relationship between **Supplier** and **Product** tables in figure 5.13, drag **SupplierId** from **Supplier** table (One side of the relationship) to **SupplierId** in **Product** table (Many side of the relationship)
- The **Edit Relationship** window will appear as shown in figure 5.14

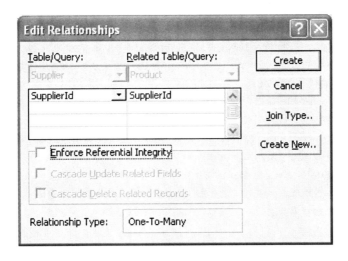

Figure 5.14

- Check the box marked **Enforce Referential Integrity** to select it. Once this box is selected, it will activate the other two boxes. Leave the other boxes unchecked.
- Click **Create**

Enforce Referential Integrity

Microsoft Access uses Referential integrity to ensure that relationships between records in related tables are valid and that you do not accidentally delete or change related data. By selecting this option Access will apply the following rules to your relationship

1. You must always enter the record on the one side of a relationship before you can enter a related record on the many side. For example, you will not be able to enter a product to the **Product** table unless there is a supplier for that product in the **Supplier** table.
2. You can not delete a record from a primary table if matching records exist in a related table. For example, you will not be able to delete records (a supplier) in **Supplier** table if there are products assigned to that supplier in the **Product** table
3. You can not change a primary key value in the primary table if that record has related records. For example, you can not change **SupplierId** in **Supplier** table if there are products assigned to that **Supplier** in the **Product** table.

When you check the box marked **Enforce Referential Integrity**, then you have two more options: **Cascade Update Related Fields** and **Cascade Delete Related Records**.

- **Cascade Update Related Fields**: If this option is chosen, the third rule of referential integrity is overridden. Any time you change the primary key of a record in the primary table, Microsoft Access will automatically update the primary key in all related tables. For example, if you change the primary key **SupplierId** in **Supplier** table (Here we are making the assumption that the primary key is not an AutoNumber) then the **SupplierId** field in **Product** table is automatically updated for every one of that supplier's products. Remember if the primary key in the table is an AutoNumber field, setting this option will have no effect because you can not change the value in an AutoNumber field.

- **Cascade Delete Related Records**: If this option is chosen, the second rule of referential integrity is overridden. Any time you delete records in the primary table, Microsoft Access automatically deletes related records in the related tables. Consider the relationship between **Customer** and **Order** tables. If you delete a customer's record from the **Customer** table, Access would automatically delete the records for every order that a customer placed. Sometime this may not be a good idea. Consider another relationship between **Order** and **OrderDetail** tables. If you are asked to delete an order and you have not checked this option, the details for that order will not be deleted in OrderDetail table. Therefore, to delete an order and its related details, you must check this option

When you are learning and experimenting with Access, it is a good idea to leave these two options unchecked. As your confidence in using Access grows, you can return and enable either one or both of them.

The next table is the **Order** table which has two foreign keys i.e. **CustomerId** and **EmployeeId**. First we will create the relationship between the **Customer** table and the **Order** table. The relationship between Customer table and Order table is one-to-many.

- To set the degree of the relationship between **Customer** and **Order**, drag **CustomerId** from **Customer** table (One side of the relationship) to **CustomerId** in **Order** table (Many side of the relationship)
- The **Edit Relationship** window will appear as shown in figure 5.15

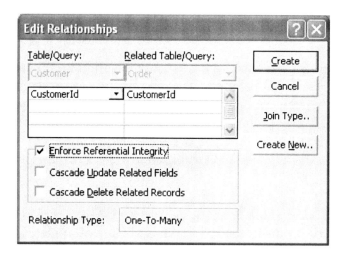

Figure 5.15

- Check the box marked **Enforce Referential Integrity** to select it. Once this box is selected, it will activate the other two boxes
- Check **Cascade Update Related Fields** box. Leave the other box unchecked.
- click **Create**

97

The other foreign key in **Order** table is the **EmployeeId**. The relationship between **Employee** table and **Order** table is one-to-many.

- To set the degree of the relationship between **Employee** and **Order**, drag **EmployeeId** from **Employee** table (One side of the relationship) to **EmployeeId** in **Order** table (Many side of the relationship)
- The **Edit Relationship** window will appear as shown in figure 5.16.

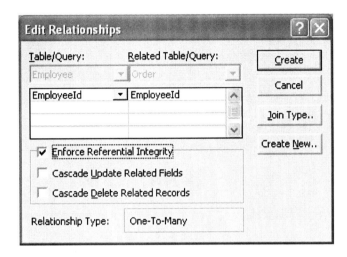

Figure 5.16

- Check the box marked **Enforce Referential Integrity** to select it. Once this box is selected, it will activate the other two boxes. Leave the other boxes unchecked.
- Click **Create**

The **Invoice** table has two foreign keys i.e. **OrderId** and **PymntMehtodId**. This means that we have to create two relationships. One between Order table and Invoice table and the other between PaymentMethod table and Invoice table.

The relationship between **Order** table and **Invoice** table is one-to-one. You can implement a one-to-one relationship between two tables if both the related fields are primary keys or have unique indexes. As OrderId is already a primary key in Order table, you need to have the indexed property for **OrderId** in Invoice table to be set to **Yes (No Duplicates)**

- Close the **Relationship** window. A dialog box will open asking if you want to save changes to the layout of relationships
- Click on **Yes**
- In main database window, click **Tables** if not selected
- Right click the **Invoice** table and then select **Design View**. You will see the screen in figure 5.17

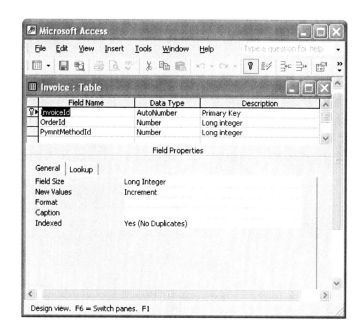

Figure 5.17

- Click on **OrderId** field and you will see the screen in figure 5.18

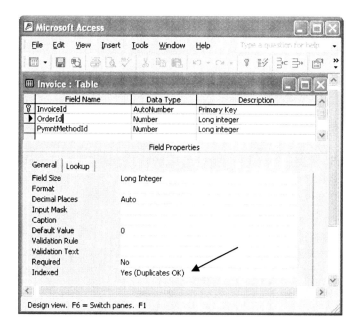

Figure 5.18

You will notice that the **Indexed** field is **Yes (Duplicates OK)**.

- Click in **Indexed** field and then click the down arrow. You will be given a choice. Select **Yes (No Duplicates)**
- Close the **Invoice** table. You will be given a choice to save changes to the design of the table

- Click **Yes** to save the changes
- Click **Tools**, select **Relationships**
- To set the degree of the relationship between **Order** and **Invoice**, drag **OrderId** from **Order** table (One side of the relationship) to **OrderId** in **Invoice** table (One side of the relationship)
- The **Edit Relationship** window will appear as shown in figure 5.19

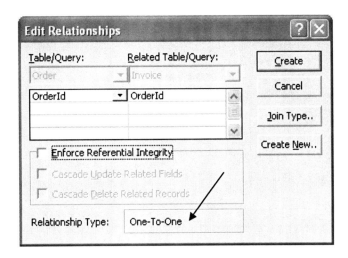

Figure 5.19

The box next to **Relationship Type**: will show One-To-One. This means that it is a one-to-one relationship

- Check the **Enforce Referential Integrity** box
- Check the **Cascade Update Related Fields** box
- Check the **Cascade Delete Related Records**
- Click **Create**

The relationship between **PaymentMethod** table and **Invoice** table is one-to-one. We have to repeat the same procedure to establish the relationship between the two tables.

- Close the **Relationship** window
- In main database window, click **Tables** if not selected
- Right click **Invoice** table and then select **Design View**. You will see the screen in figure 5.20

Figure 5.20

- Click in **PymntMethodId** field and you will see the screen in figure 5.21

Figure 5.21

- You will notice that the **Indexed** field is **Yes (Duplicates OK)**. Click in **Indexed** field and then click on the down arrow. You will be given a choice. Select **Yes (No Duplicates)**
  - Close the **Invoice** table. You will be given a choice to save changes to the design of the table
  - Click **Yes** to save the change
- Click **Tools**, select **Relationships**
- To set the degree of the relationship between **PaymentMethod** and **Invoice** tables, drag **PymntMethodId** from **PaymentMethod** table (One side of the relationship) to **PymntMethodId** in **Invoice** table (One side of the relationship)
- The **Edit Relationship** window will appear as shown in figure 5.22

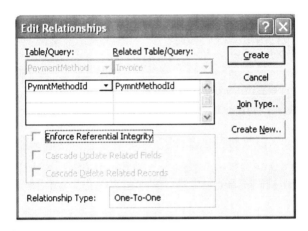

Figure 5.22

The box next to **Relationship Type**: will show One-To-One. This means that it is a one-to-one relationship

- Check the **Enforce Referential Integrity** box
- Check the **Cascade Update Related Fields** box
- Check the **Cascade Delete Related Records** box
- Click **Create**

The last remaining table with foreign keys is the **OrderDetail** table. It has two foreign keys i.e. **OrderId** and **ProductId**. We will deal with the relationship between **Order** table and **OrderDetail** table first. The relationship between Order table and OrderDetail table is one-to-many.

- To set the degree of relationship between **Order** and **OrderDetail**, drag **OrderId** from **Order** table (One side of the relationship) to **OrderId** in **OrderDetail** table (Many side of the relationship)
- The **Edit Relationship** window in figure 4.23 will appear

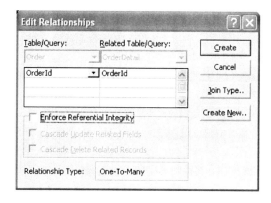

Figure 5.23

The box next to **Relationship Type**: will show One-To-Many. This means that it is a one-to-many relationship

- Check the **Enforce Referential Integrity** box
- Check the **Cascade Delete Related Records** box
- Click **Create**

The next foreign key in **OrderDetail** table is the **ProductId** from **Product** table. The relationship between **Product** table and **OrderDetail** table is one-to-many.

- To set the degree of the relationship between **Product** and **OrderDetail**, drag **ProductId** from **Product** table (One side of the relationship) to **ProductId** in **OrderDetail** table (Many side of the relationship)
- The **Edit Relationship** window in figure 5.24 will appear

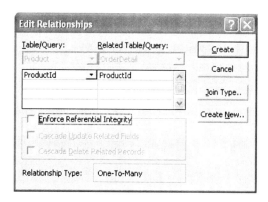

Figure 5.24

The box next to **Relationship Type**: will show One-To-Many. This means that it is a one-to-many relationship

- Click in **Enforce Referential Integrity** box and leave the other options unchecked as we do not want to cascade the other changes
- Click **Create**

After creating the Relationship between tables, my Relationships window looks as shown in figure 5.25.

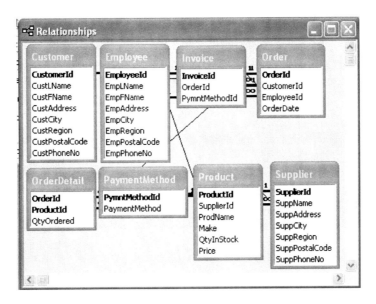

Figure 5.25

As you can see, the Relationships window in figure 5.25 is not very clear. To make it clear, move the tables in Relationships window around so that they look as shown in figure 5.26. You can move a table by clicking the top of the table and then dragging it in the desired direction in the relationship window.

Looking at figure 5.26, you would notice that Access places "1" on one end of the line and the infinity symbol (many) on the other end of the line linking two tables. This shows that one-to-many relationship exists between the two tables. You would also notice that some of the tables are linked by lines which end up in the symbol "1" on both sides. This shows that the relationship between the two tables is one-to-one.

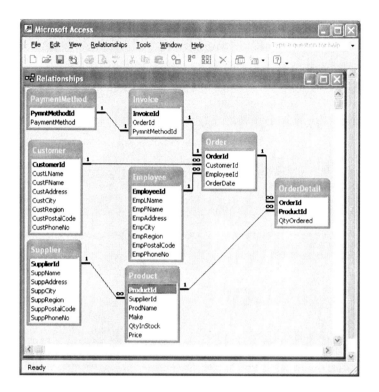

Figure 5.26

- Close the **Relationships** window. This will bring the screen in figure 5.27

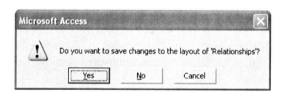

Figure 5.27

- Click **Yes** to save the layout. This will bring you back to the main database window

Chapter 6

Creating forms

In the last chapter, first we created a database. Then we created tables in the database according to the ER diagram that was developed in the previous chapters. Finally we created the relationship between the tables. Now how one should enter data into these tables? You can enter data directly in to a table in datasheet view as shown in figure 6.1 or you can use a form to enter data as shown in figure 6.2. Entering data in datasheet view allows you to view and edit the records all on one screen. Datasheet view is good for testing purposes when you are developing a new database. Entering data in form view allows you to view and edit data records one at a time. A form view is a much easier way of entering data for end users. You can design easy and intuitive forms for use with one table or you can build them to service more than one table at a time. In this chapter, we are going to discuss how to create the right kind of forms for our database.

		EmployeeId	EmpLName	EmpFName	EmpAddress	EmpCity	EmpRegion	EmpPostalCode	EmpPhoneNo
	+	1	Lam	Tom	10 Leslie St	Markham	Ontario	M1E3H6	416-123-4567
	+	2	Francis	Jody	11 Bayview St	Clayton	Manitoba	G3G5U8	417-123-3456
	+	3	Chiu	Jim	5 Front St	Toronto	Ontario	T9T4H7	418-123-4567
*		AutoNumber)							

Record: 3 of 3

Figure 6.1 Datasheet view

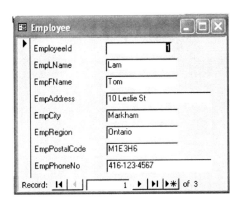

Figure 6.2 Form View

During the finding of user requirements in chapter 4, we asked the following question about an employee.

You: What kind of things do you do with the information on an Employee?
Owner: I need to enter details about each new employee and delete it when they leave. I also need an employee's name on each invoice. The main purpose of this exercise is to

track down who made the sale. At the end of year, employees are paid bonuses according to their performance.

Possible form: To maintain (enter, update and delete) data on employees.

The answer to this question is helping us in determining what kind of form is needed. Now let us create a form that can do this function.

- In main database window, select **Forms** as shown in figure 6.3
- Click **New**. A new window will appear as shown in figure 6.4

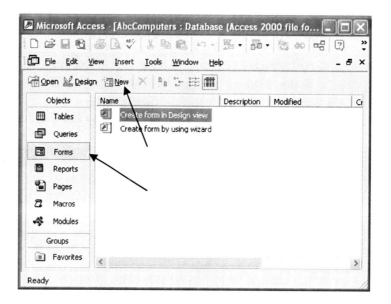

Figure 6.3

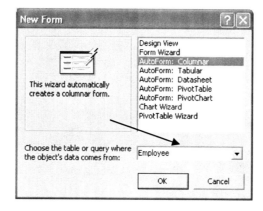

Figure 6.4

- In the **New Form** window select **AutoForm: Columnar**
- Select the **Employee** table from the drop down list and click **OK**. You will get a screen as shown in figure 6.5

107

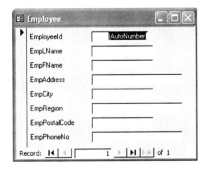

Figure 6.5

- Close the window and you will get a screen as shown in figure 6.6

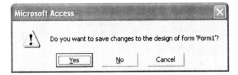

Figure 6.6

- Click **Yes** and this will bring another screen as shown in figure 6.7

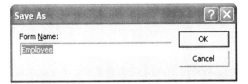

Figure 6.7

- In the **Save As** box type **FrmEmployee** and click **OK**.

The AutoForm wizard will create the form and return to main database window as shown in figure 6.8.

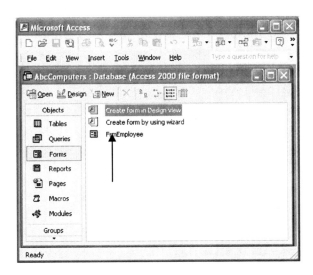

Figure 6.8

Adding a record to a Form

- In the main database window in figure 6.8, double click **FrmEmployee**. This will open the form as shown in figure 6.9. You can use this window to add new employees into the Employee table

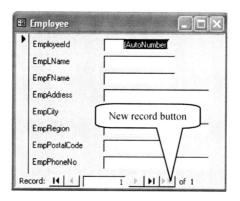

Figure 6.9

Let us add an employee to the table through this form. In figure 6.9, the new record button (a star next to an arrow head) is not showing black because there is no record in the table.

- Tab out of the EmployeeId field and enter the employee details as following
- In EmpLName, type Chiu
- Tab out to EmpFName and type Jim
- Tab out to EmpAddress and type 5 Front St
- Tab out to EmpCity and type Toronto
- Tab out to EmpRegion and type Ontario
- Tab out to EmpPostalCode and type T9T 4H7
- Tab out to EmpPhoneNo and type 418-123-4567
- Click the new record button and it will save the record to the table
- Enter another record as following
- In EmpLName, type Francis
- In EmpFName, type Jodhy
- In EmpAddress, type 123 Victoria St
- In EmpCity, type Halifax
- In EmpRegion, type Nova Scotia
- In EmpPostalCode, type K7Y 1J1
- In EmpPhoneNo, type 416-123-5678
- Close the Employee form and the record will be saved to the Employee table

Deleting a record in a Form

Suppose your boss asked you to delete Jim Chiu's record. He is not working with the company any more.

- In the main database window, select **Forms**
- Double click **FrmEmployee**
- Find Jim Chiu's record using the left and right arrow buttons. Once you find the record then click the **Delete Record** button on the toolbar as shown in figure 6.10

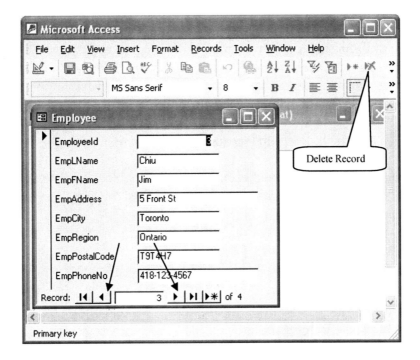

Figure 6.10

- A message will appear as shown in figure 6.11. Click **Yes** to delete Jim's record

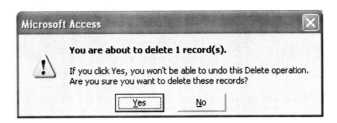

Figure 6.11

You successfully deleted a record from the **Employee** table.

- Close the Form

So far with the help of this form you can add, edit and delete an employee. This was one of the requirements of Mr. Brown. The other requirement was to have the employee name on the invoice. We will deal with this requirement in a chapter dedicated for reports.

Creating a Customer Form

In chapter 4, the second question about each entity in the user requirements deals with the forms issue. As this chapter is dedicated to creating forms for our database, we will be working on this question for each entity. The Customer entity is next, so let us work on this one.

You: What kind of things do you do with the information on a Customer?
Owner: We need to enter details about each new customer. This information is used for warranty purposes. We should also be able to change the information for an existing customer. I also need to list the names of the customers who are the most valuable.

Possible form: To maintain (enter, update and delete) data on customers.

The owner needs to enter details about each new customer. So we need to create a form that can do that. The process of creating this form is almost the same as the one we did for the Employee.

- In main database window, select **Forms**
- Click on **New** and the **New Form** window will appear
- Select **AutoForm: Columnar**
- Select the **Customer** table from the drop down list and click **OK** and you will see a screen as shown in figure 6.12

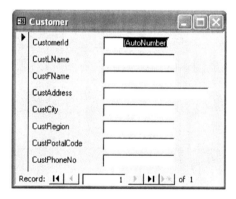

Figure 6.12

- Close the window and then you will be prompted "Do you want to save changes to the design of form 'Form1'"
- Click **Yes** to save the changes
- In the **Save As** box type **FrmCustomer** and click **OK**.

The AutoForm wizard creates a Customer form.

- Double click **FrmCustomer** in forms window and you will see the screen in figure 6.13

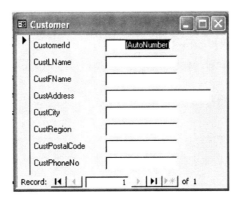

Figure 6.13

Let us add a customer to the Customer table using this form.

- Tab out of the **CustomerId** field and enter the customer details as following
- In **CustLName**, type Doe
- Tab out to **CustFName** and type Jhon
- Tab out to **CustAddress** and type 15 Front St
- Tab out to **CustCity** and type Toronto
- Tab out to **CustRegion** and type Ontario
- Tab out to **CustPostalCode** and type T9T 4H7
- Tab out to **CustPhoneNo** and type 418-398-4567
- Close the Form and the record will be saved to the Customer table

With the help of this form you can add, edit and delete a customer's details. The last part of Mr. Brown's statement "I also need to list the names of the customers who are the most valuable" deals with creating a report. We will deal with this part in a chapter dedicated for reports. We move on to the next question related to Supplier entity.

You: What kind of things do you do with the information on a Supplier?
Owner: I need to enter details about a supplier. Some time if a customer enquires about the availability of a new product or a sold out product, one of my employees may call the supplier about the availability of that product.

Possible form: To maintain (enter, update and delete) data on a supplier.

The owner needs to enter details about each Supplier. We need to create a form that can do that. The process of creating this form is almost the same as the one we did for the Employee. We will be loading data into the Supplier table through this form.

Creating a Supplier Form

- In the database window, select **Forms** and click on **New**
- In the **New Form** window select **AutoForm: Columnar**
- Select the **Supplier** table from the drop down list and click **OK**

- Close the window and then you will be prompted "Do you want to save changes to the design of form 'Form1'"
- Click **Yes** to save the changes
- In the **Save As** box type **FrmSupplier** and Click **OK**

The AutoForm wizard creates a form.

- Double click **FrmSupplier** in form window and you will see the screen in figure 6.14

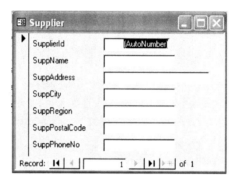

Figure 6.14

Let us add a few suppliers to the table through this form

- Click in **SuppName** and type Teknet Computers
- Tab out to **SuppAddress** and type 100 Lawrence Ave
- Tab out to **SuppCity** and type Halifax
- Tab out to **SuppRegion** and type Nova Scotia
- Tab out to **SuppPostalCode** and type N1H 3K4
- Tab out to **SuppPhoneNo** and type 905-123-1234

- Click on the new record button (a star next to an arrow head)
- Click in **SuppName** and type TNG Computers
- Tab out to **SuppAddress** and type 50 Eglinton Ave
- Tab out to **SuppCity** and type Markham
- Tab out to **SuppRegion** and type Manitoba
- Tab out to **SuppPostalCode** and type J1K 3N5
- Tab out to **SuppPhoneNo** and type 416-123-1234

- Click on the new record button (a star next to an arrow head)
- Click in **SuppName** and type Hitek Computers
- Tab out to **SuppAddress** and type 150 College St
- Tab out to **SuppCity** and type Toronto
- Tab out to **SuppRegion** and type Ontario
- Tab out to **SuppPostalCode** and type M1K 6J7

- Tab out to **SuppPhoneNo** and type 647-123-1234
- Close the form and all the records will be saved to the **Supplier** table
- In main database window select **Tables** as shown in figure 6.15

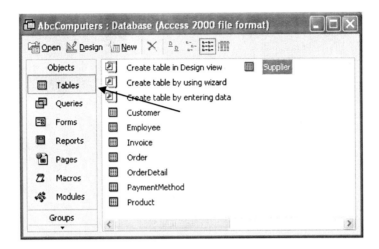

Figure 6.15

- Double click **Supplier** and you will see a screen as shown in figure 6.16. Each supplier is assigned a SupplierId

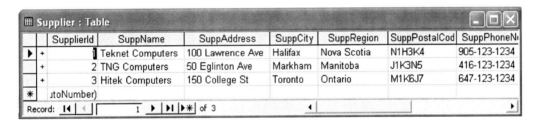

Figure 6.16

- Close this window

So far we created three forms and each one is based on a single table. Each form has fields from one table and is on one side of the relationship as shown in figure 6.17

Consider you want to create a form to enter details for a product. Now according to the relationship diagram in figure 6.17, there is relationship between table **Product** and table **Supplier**. You can not have a product without knowing its supplier in the database. This means that we are dealing with two tables. The Product table has the primary key field from Supplier table. In such a situation where a table has fields from two or more tables, it is a good idea to first create a multi table query in which fields from two or more tables can be combined together. Once the query is created then you can create a form based on that query. We will leave the creation of the rest of the forms until we discuss queries.

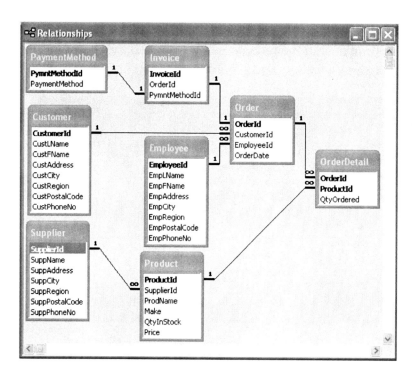

Figure 6.17

Chapter 7

Queries

In the previous chapters, we created a database. To manipulate the data in the database, we need some kind of a tool. Queries is one of the most important tool available in Microsoft Access to convert raw data into useful information. Queries can perform a number of different functions. They can be used to look at data, add, edit or delete data. Queries can perform calculations and return results. The values in a field can be summed, the number of values counted, averages calculated and so on. They can also be used as a record source for a form or report. Queries is one of the most important reason behind the popularity of relational database systems.

Types of query

There are six different types of queries in Access as shown in figure 7.1. They are

- Select query
- Crosstab query
- Make-table query
- Update query
- Append query
- Delete query

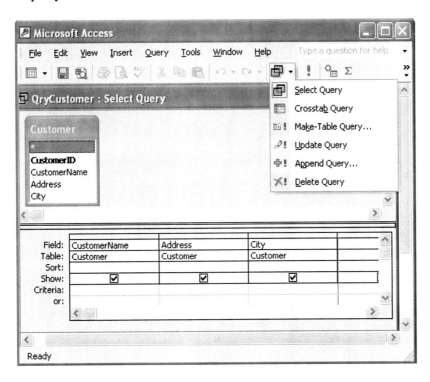

Figure 7.1 Shows different kind of queries available in Microsoft Access

To create a query, you need to take the following steps

- Find out what tables you need for the query
- Find out what fields you need in the query
- What criteria needed to produce the required result
- Running the query
- Saving the query

Query involving one table

We start with the simplest query which is the select query. It retrieves data from one or more tables and displays the results in a datasheet.

Let us create a query that lists all the suppliers for ABC Computers. We need the Supplier table for this query.

- In the main database window click **Queries**, you will see a screen as shown in figure 7.2

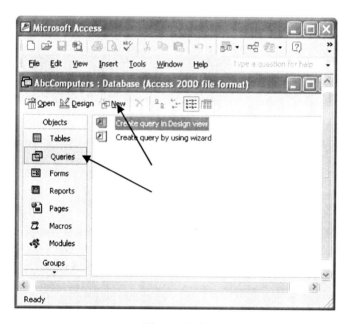

Figure 7.2

- Click **New**. A screen as shown in figure 7.3 will appear

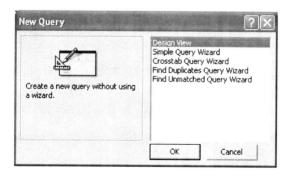

Figure 7.3

- Select **Design View** and then click **Ok**
- The **Show table** window will appear on the top of **Select Query** window as shown in figure 7.4

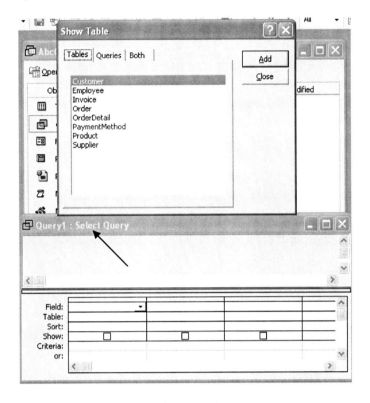

Figure 7.4

- Select **Supplier** table and then click **Add**
- Click **Close**. The **Supplier** table will appear in the **Query Design View** as shown in figure 7.5

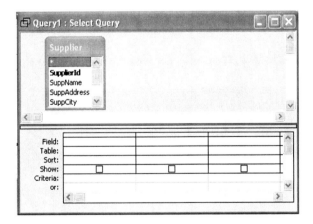

Figure 7.5

The window in figure 7.5 is divided into two portions. The upper portion displays each selected table used in the query. Each selected table displays a list of fields that you can add to the query. The lower portion displays the design grid where you can design the query. This portion is also called the QBE (Query By Example) grid. This section consists of five rows

Field   Shows the field selected from the table for the query
Table   Shows the name of the table containing the selected field
Sort   Offers ascending, descending sort options
Show   Allows you to show or hide fields in the output
Criteria   Allows you to enter criteria for the search

- Place all the fields in **Supplier** table in query grid by double clicking each field. You will get a query grid as shown in figure 7.6

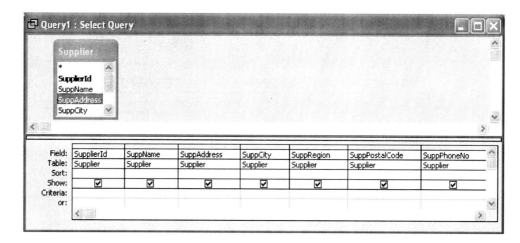

Figure 7.6

Do not change anything else as we want all the information about the suppliers for ABC Computers.

- **Close** the query window. You will get a screen as shown in figure 7.7

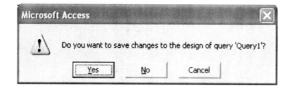

Figure 7.7

- Click **Yes** and the screen in figure 7.8 will appear

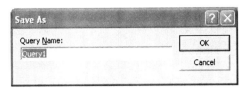

Figure 7.8

- Type **QryListSuppliers** in the **Save As** box. Click **Ok**
- You will get the screen in figure 7.9. Query **QryListSuppliers** is listed in the window

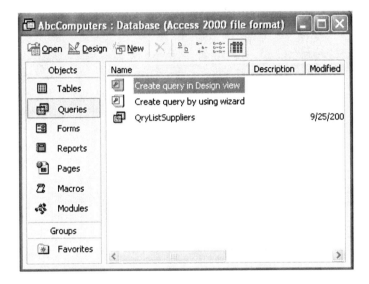

Figure 7.9

- Double click **QryListSuppliers** and you will see the screen in figure 7.10

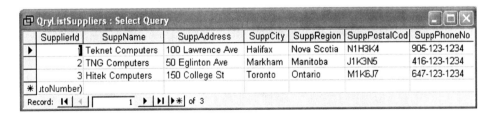

Figure 7.10

As you can see, ABC Computers has three suppliers. If you recall from last chapter, we added these suppliers through a supplier form.

- Close the window

Query involving multiple tables

In the last chapter when it came to creating a form for product, we skipped it because it needed data from two tables. We said that it is better to create a query on the two tables and then create a form on that query. Now let us find out what tables should be considered for this query.

- On the toolbar, select **Tools, Relationships**

You will see the screen in figure 7.11. The **Product** table and the **Supplier** table are linked by **SupplierId** field. To add a product to the Product table, first we have to know the supplier for that product. So we need the Supplier table and the Product table for this query.

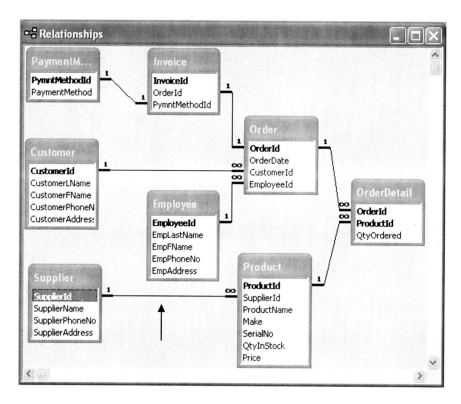

Figure 7.11

- Close the **Relationships** window
- While still in **Queries** window, Double click **Create query in Design view**
- You will see the screen in figure 7.12

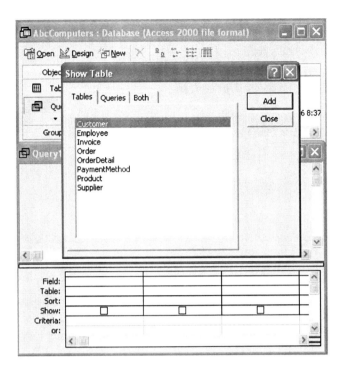

Figure 7.12

- Double click **Supplier** and then **Product.** This will add the two tables to the QBE grid.
- Click **Close** and this will bring the screen in figure 7.13

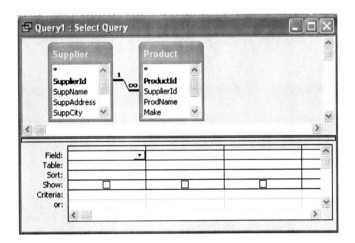

Figure 7.13

You will notice a line connecting SupplierId in Supplier table to a SupplierId in Product table. This shows that a one-to- many relationship already exists between the two tables.

- In **Supplier** table, double click **SuppName** field. This will add **SuppName** field to the QBE grid

- In **Product** table, double click all the fields. This will add all the fields in **Product** table to the QBE grid.

You will get a screen as shown in figure7.14

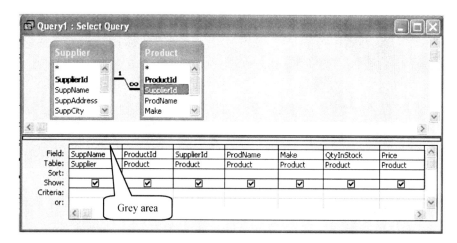

Figure 7.14

We want to move **SuppName** field towards right so that it is between **SupplierId** and **ProdName**.

- Click the grey area above **SuppName**. This will highlight SuppName field
- Click again in the same area and do not release the mouse button. Drag the SuppName towards right until the vertical black bar is between **SupplierId** and **ProdName**. Release the mouse button. You will see a screen as shown in figure 7.15

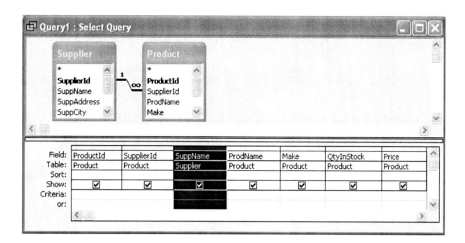

Figure 7.15

- Click any where in the empty space in QBE grid to get rid of the highlighting of **SuppName** field
- Close the window. This will bring the screen shown in figure 7.16.

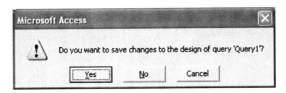

Figure 7.16

- Click **Yes**. This will bring the screen in figure 7.17

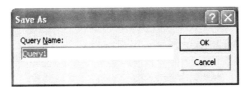

Figure 7.17

- Type **QryProduct** in **Save As** box
- Click **Ok**. This will create the query
- Double click **QryProduct** in **Queries** window. You will see the screen in figure 7.18

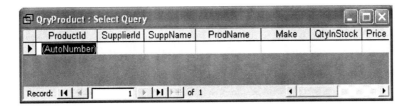

Figure 7.18

As you can see in figure 7.18, the query is getting some information from Supplier table (SuppName) and the rest of the information from product table. Next we want to create a form that can be used for entering information for a product. This form will be using QryProduct as its source.

- Close the **QryProduct** window
- In the main database window, select **Forms** and then click **New**
- In the **New Form** window select **AutoForm: Columnar**
- From the drop down list select **QryProduct** as shown in figure 7.19

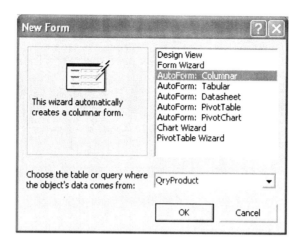

Figure 7.19

- Click **OK**. You will get the screen in figure 7.20

Figure 7.20

- Close the window and you will get the screen in figure 7.21

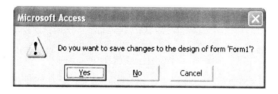

Figure 7.21

- Click **Yes** and you will get the screen in figure 7.22

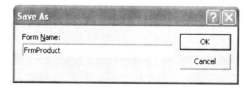

Figure 7.22

- Type **FrmProduct** in **Save As** box and click **Ok**

This will create FrmProduct as shown in figure 7.23.

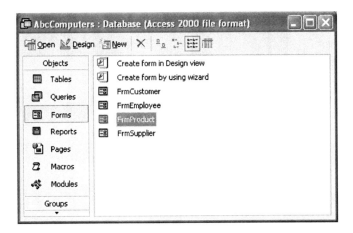

Figure 7.23

- Double click **FrmProduct** and you will get the screen in figure 7.24

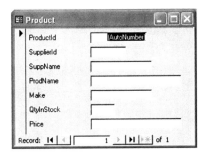

Figure 7.24

FrmProduct gets supplier name (SuppName field) information from **Supplier** table. It would be a good idea to add a drop down menu for SuppName field to FrmProduct. This will enable us to select one of the suppliers available in the Supplier table. For any new supplier that is not in the Supplier table, you must add the supplier first to the **Supplier** table through FrmSupplier and then you can add that supplier to the **Product** table through this form.

- Close the form
- In the main database window select **Forms** if not selected
- Right click **FrmProduct**
- Select **Design View** and you will get the screen in figure 7.25

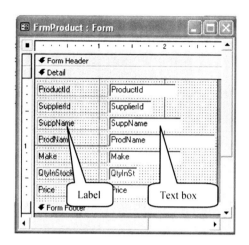

Figure 7.25

- Click **SuppName** label and press **Delete**
- Click **SuppName** text box and press **Delete**
- Click **SupplierId** label and press **Delete**
- Click **SupplierId** text box and press **Delete**

You will get a screen as shown in figure 7.26

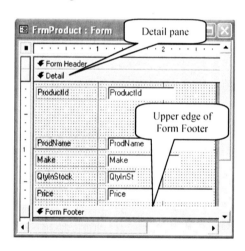

Figure 7.26

- Press the **Shift** key and then click on label and text box for **ProdName, Make, QtyInStock** and **Price**. This will select all these fields. Release the **Shift** key
- Move the selected fields upward towards **ProductId** field and leave enough empty space for one field as shown in figure 7.27
- Click anywhere in the empty space to deselect the selected controls
- Move the upper edge of **Form Footer** upward and stop under the **Price** field
- Right click anywhere in the empty space in **Detail** pane and select **Toolbox**. You will get a screen shown in figure 7.27
- In the Control **Toolbox**, make sure that the **Control Wizard** button is depressed

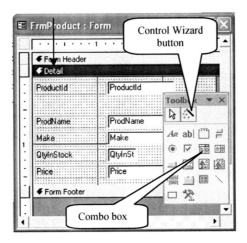

Figure 7.27

- Click the **Combo box** icon and then click in the empty space between **ProductId** and **ProdName**. We want the combo box to appear in this empty space. This will start **Combo box wizard** as shown in figure 7.28

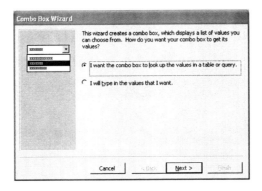

Figure 7.28

- Select **I want the combo box to look up the values in a table or query** and click **Next**. You will get the screen in figure 7.29

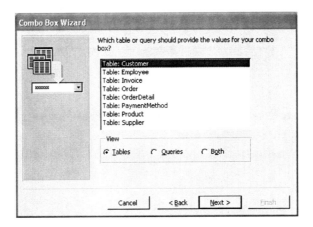

Figure 7.29

- Click **Table: Supplier** and click **Next**. You will get a screen as shown in figure 7.30

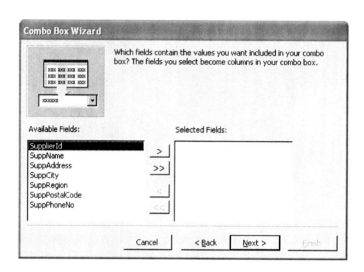

Figure 7.30

- Add **SuppName** to the **Selected Fields** and click **Next**. You will get the screen in figure 7.31

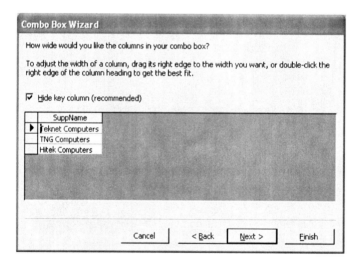

Figure 7.31

- Adjust **SuppName** column label by dragging it towards right at the top in case it is not wide enough for **SuppName**
- Leave **Hide key column** checked and click **Next**. You will get a screen as shown in figure 7.32

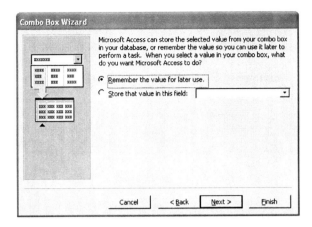

Figure 7.32

- Select **Store that value in this field** and then select **SupplierId** from the drop down menu
- Click **Next** and you will get a screen shown in figure 7.33

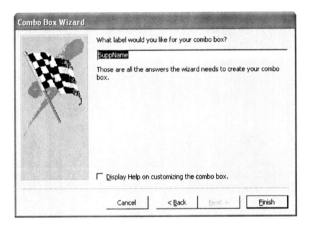

Figure 7.33

- Type **Supplier** in the box
- Click **Finish**. You will get a screen shown in figure 7.34

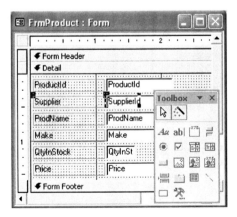

Figure 7.34

- Close the **Toolbox** window.
- Close **FrmProduct** window and you will get a screen in figure 7.35

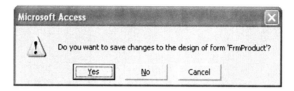

Figure 7.35

- Click **Yes** and the screen will disappear

To test the newly created form, let us add some data into Product table through this form.

- In **Forms** window, double click **FrmProduct**. You will get a screen in figure 7.36

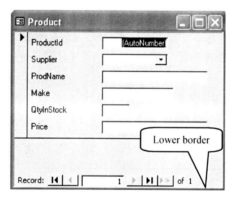

Figure 7.36

- To adjust the size of the window, bring the mouse pointer to the lower border of the form, when it becomes a two headed arrow, drag the border upward so that it looks as shown in figure 7.37

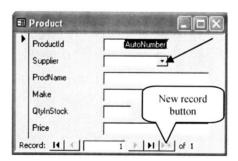

Figure 7.37

- Click the **Supplier** drop down arrow and select Teknet Computers
- In **ProdName** field type 80 GB Hard disk

- In **Make** field type Maxtor
- In **QtyInStock** field type 5
- In **Price** field type 100
- Click the **New record** button to add another product
- Click the **Supplier** drop down list and select TNG Computers
- In **ProdName**, type 19 inch LCD monitor
- In **Make**, type Fujitech
- In **QtyInStock**, type 7
- In **Price**, type 500
- Close the form
- In the main database window, Select **Tables**
- Double click **Product** table and you will get a screen as shown in figure 7.38

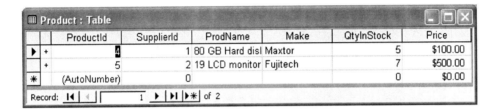

Figure 7.38

As you can see in figure 7.38, product information has been entered into Product table. A ProductId and a SupplierId has also been assigned automatically to the product. You may be wondering where is SuppName field. The Product table does not have any SuppName field and references a supplier through a SupplierId. We added the supplier (SuppName) drop down list to FrmProduct because it is easy for humans to remember a name instead of a number. After selecting the supplier name, the Combo box added the right SupplierId to the Product table.

- Close the **Product** table window

Chapter 8

Advanced Forms

You can create a simple data entry form on a table or a query by using the form wizard. Some of the most useful forms simply can not be created by a form wizard. They are complex and require careful planning and effort. Before building a complex form, determine what information the form will need and in what order you will build its parts. The focus of this chapter is the planning and construction of such a complex form.

Designing the Main form

Here we are going to create the main form which is the Order form. This is the most useful and complex of all the forms that we are going to create. Many databases need this kind of a form.

The Order form should be able to do the following functions

- Look up a customer in the Customer table and then enter the correct CustomerId for the customer into the Order table
- Enter a new customer in case the customer is not in the Customer table
- Look up an employee in the Employee table and then enter the correct EmployeeId for the employee into the Order table
- Enter the ordered items into the OrderDetail table
- Enter payment information
- Print an invoice for the customer
- Display an order's total

Now a good plan to create such a form would be to create a combination of forms and a report to print the invoice. We can achieve such a goal by creating an Order form that will have the following

- A main form that enters all the information needed in the Order table including the Customer information and the employee name
- A command button that can enter information for a new customer
- A subform that enters the items being ordered into the OrderDetail table
- A subform that enters the payment information
- A command button that can print a report as an invoice

Figure 8.1 shows the kind of Order form that we want to create. As you can see that the outer form is the main form and the subforms are embedded within the main form. A subform is a form within a form. You can embed as many subforms in a main form as you want but you can nest forms only up to two deep. Using a subform within a main form allows you to display and edit records in different tables in the same form.

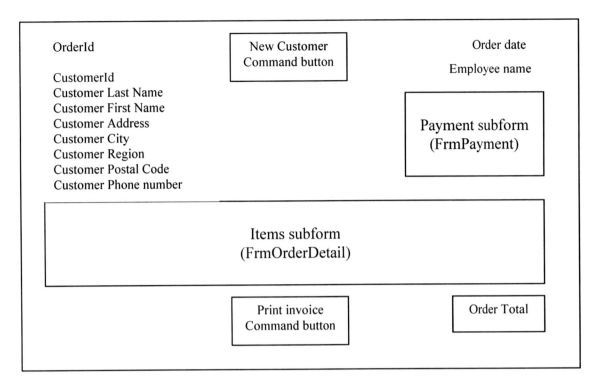

Figure 8.1 Order form layout

To link a subform to a main form, you need a linking field that is shared by both forms. We will discuss this when we add the subforms into the main form.

Let us create the main form which is the Order form. We call this form as FrmOrder.

Creating FrmOrder

We need a query specifically created for the Order form. We call this query as QryOrder.

- In **Queries** window, click the **New** button
- Double click **Design View**
- Add **Customer** table, **Order** table and **Employee** table to the query window
- Click **Close**

The **Customer** table and **Order** table are joined by **CustomerId**. The **Order** table and **Employee** table are joined by **EmployeeId** as shown in figure 8.2

- From **Order** table add OrderId, CustomerId, EmployeeId and OrderDate fields to the QBE grid by double clicking each field
- From **Customer** table add CustLName, CustFName, CustAddress, CustCity, CustRegion, CustPostalCode and CustPhoneNo fields to the QBE grid
- From **Employee** table add EmpLName and EmpFName fields to the QBE grid
- Close the window. You will be asked if you want to save changes to the design of the query
- Click **Yes** and save the query as **QryOrder**

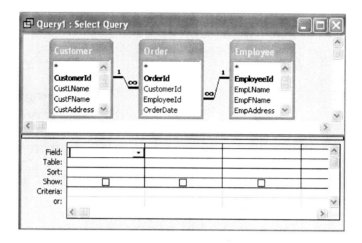

Figure 8.2

Next we want to create a form that is based on this query

- In the Database window select **Forms** and then click on **New**
- In the **New Form** window select **Autoform: Columnar**
- Select **QryOrder** from the drop down list and click **Ok**

You will see a screen as shown in figure 8.3

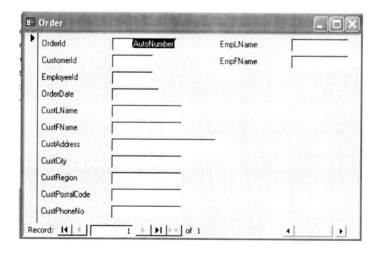

Figure 8.3

- Close the form. You will be asked if you want to save changes to the design of the form
- Click **Yes** and save the form as **FrmOrder**
- In Forms window, Click **FrmOrder**
- Click the **Design** button in database window to open the form in design view. You will see a screen as shown in figure 8.4

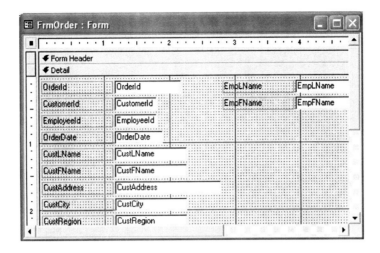

Figure 8.4

- Maximize the window and you will get a screen as shown in figure 8.5

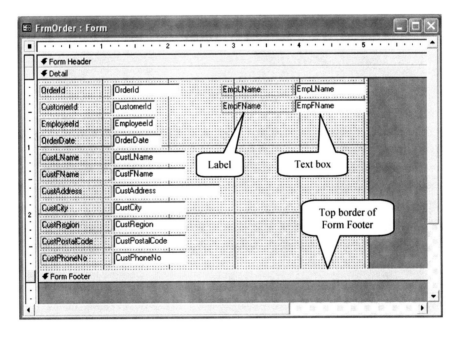

Figure 8.5

- Bring the mouse pointer to the top border of **Form Footer** bar. When the pointer becomes a two headed arrow, drag the border downward until you can see all controls and enough space for Items subform as shown in figure 8.6

In figure 8.5, there is a **Label** and a **Text box** for each field on the form. In Access, any object on a form is called Control. There are many types of controls. Some of the controls are labels, text boxes, list boxes, combo boxes, radio buttons and command buttons.

- Bring the mouse pointer to the right edge of the form grid. When the pointer becomes a two headed arrow, drag toward right until there is enough space for Payment subform as shown in figure 8.6

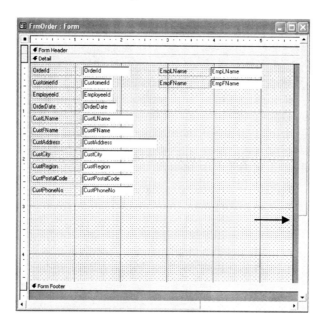

Figure 8.6

- Press the **Shift** key and then click **Label** and **Text box** for **EmpLName** and **EmpFName**. This will select the four controls
- Move the selected controls (by dragging) downward and towards right until there is enough space for **OrderDate** and **EmployeeId** controls as shown in figure 8.7
- Click any where in the empty space in form grid to deselect the four controls
- Press **Shift** key and then click **Label** and **Text box** for **OrderDate**
- Move the selected controls to the empty space just created as shown in figure 8.7
- Click anywhere in the empty space in form grid to deselect the two controls
- Press **Shift** key and then click **Label** and **Text box** for **EmployeeId**
- Move the selected controls to the empty space just below **OrderDate** controls as shown in figure 8.7
- Click anywhere in the empty space in form grid to deselect the two controls
- Press **Shift** key and then click **Label** and **Text box** for **CustLName**, **CustFName, CustAddress, CustCity, CustRegion, CustPostalCode** and **CustPhoneNo**. This will select all these controls
- Move the selected controls upward toward **CustomerId** as shown in figure 8.7
- Click anywhere in the empty space in form grid to deselect the controls

Your form should look as shown in figure 8.7

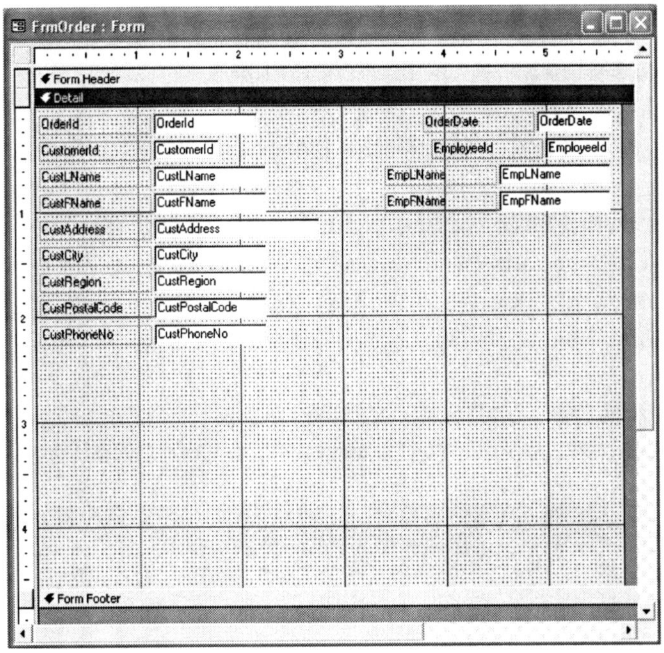

Figure 8.7

- Close the form and save the changes to the design of the form

Creating Items Subform

We want to create Items subform which will be a part of the main Order form. This form will be based on a query called QryOrderDetail specifically created for this form. This subform and its underlying query will enter ProdName, Make, Price, QtyOrdered and Item Total for customer's order.

Let us look at the relationship between the three tables as shown in figure 8.8. This query must include OrderId from OrderDetail table so that the subform can later be linked to the main form (FrmOrder). We also need ProductId from OrderDetail table to link OrderDetail table to Product table. A new field called **Item Total** will also be added to this form that multiplies the **Price** of a specific product to the **QtyOrdered** by the customer to get the total dollar amount for that product.

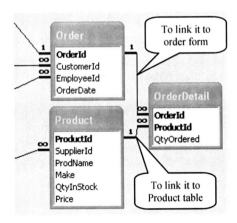

Figure 8.8

- In the **Queries** window, click the **New** button
- Double click **Design View**
- Add **Product** table and **OrderDetail** table to the query window and then click **Close**
- From **OrderDetail** table, add OrderId, ProductId and QtyOrdered to the QBE grid
- From **Product** table, add ProdName, Make and Price to the QBE grid
- In the last empty field on the right, type **Item Total: [price]*[qtyordered]** and check the Show box as shown in figure 8.9

This will give us another field called **Item Total** which is the result of multiplying the **Price** field from Product table and **QtyOrdered** field from OrderDetail table.

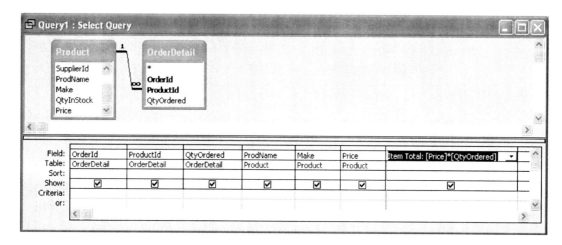

Figure 8.9

- Close the query and save it as **QryOrderDetail**

Next we are going to create a form based on this query

- In the Database Window select **Forms** and then click **New**
- In the New Form window select **AutoForm: Datasheet**
- Select **QryOrderDetail** from the drop down list and click **OK**. You will get a screen as shown in figure 8.10
- Close the form and save it as **FrmOrderDetail**

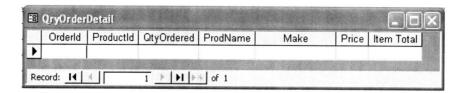

Figure 8.10

- In **Forms** window, click **FrmOrderDetail** and then click **Design**

- Maximize the window. You will get a screen as shown in figure 8.11

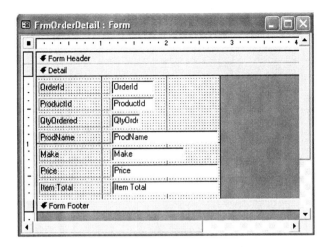

Figure 8.11

- Delete the **label** and **text box** for **OrderId**.

We need OrderId in query QryOrderDetail to link FrmOrderDetail with FrmOrder but we do not need OrderId on this form

- Delete the **label** and **text box** for **ProdName**. You will get a screen as shown in figure 8.12

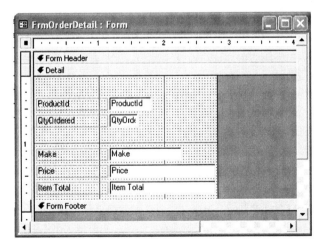

Figure 8.12

We need ProdName field on this form but it would be better to select ProdName from a list. Therefore, we would replace the label and text box for ProdName with a Combo box. This combo box will look up ProdName in the Product table and then enter your selection to the OrderDetail table

- Move the **label** and **text box** for **ProductId** to the top as shown in figure 8.13

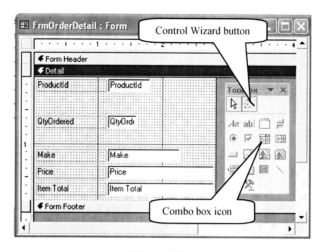

Figure 8.13

- Right click anywhere in the empty space in **Detail** pane and select **Toolbox**
- Make sure that the **Control Wizard** button in Toolbox is depressed as shown in figure 8.13
- Click the **Combo box** icon in the Toolbox and then click in the empty space between **ProductId** and **QtyOrdered**. We want the combo box to appear here. This will start the Combo box wizard
- Select "**I want the combo box to look up the values in a table or query**" and click **Next**
- Select **Table: Product** and click **Next**
- Add **ProdName** into the **Selected Fields** and click **Next**
- Adjust **ProdName** column label so that it is wide enough for the product name. Leave the **Hide Key column** checked and click **Next**
- Click **Store that value in this field:** Select **ProductId** from the drop down list and then click **Next**
- Name the combo box label as **Product** and click **Finish**. You will get a product combo box as shown in figure 8.14
- Close the **Toolbox** window if it still there
- Press the **Shift** key and then click **label** and **text box** for **QtyOrdered**
- Move the selected controls down to make room for **Make** controls
- Click anywhere in the empty space in form grid to deselect the two controls
- Press the **Shift** key and then click **label** and **text box** for **Make**
- Move the selected controls to the empty space below **Product** combo box
- Click anywhere in the empty space in form grid to deselect the two controls
- Press the **Shift** key and then click **label** and **text box** for **QtryOrdered**
- Move the selected controls down so that there is enough space for **Price**
- Click anywhere in the empty space in form grid to deselect the two controls
- Press the **Shift** key and then click the **label** and **text box** for **Price**
- Move the selected controls to the empty space below **Make**
- Click anywhere to deselect the two controls
- Click the **label** and **text box** for **Item Total** and move it up just under **QtyOrdered** as shown in figure 8.14

- Bring the mouse pointer to the top border of the **Form Footer** bar. When the pointer becomes a two headed arrow, drag the border upward towards **Item Total**. The final screen should look as shown in figure 8.14

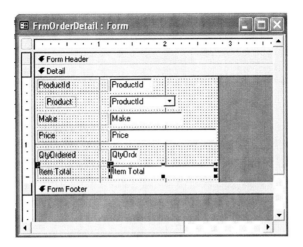

Figure 8.14

- Click the **Datasheet** tab on the Toolbar as shown in figure 8.15. This will bring the Datasheet view of the form as shown in figure 8.16

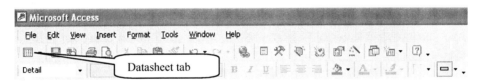

Figure 8.15

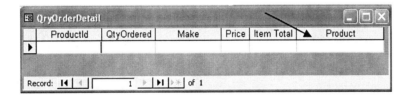

Figure 8.16

- Maximize the window so that you can see all the fields

Next we want to align the columns from left to right as ProductId, Product, Make, Price, QtyOrdered and Item Total

- Click on **Product** (column label) once. This will highlight the Product column
- Click the Product column label again and do not release the mouse button. Move the mouse towards left until you get a black vertical line between **ProductId** and **QtyOrdered** and then release the mouse button. Now Product should be the second column in the row as shown in figure 8.17

142

- Apply the same technique and arrange all the columns next to each other as shown in figure 8.17

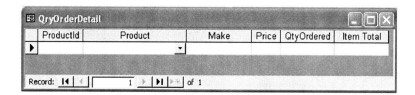

Figure 8.17

As you can see in figure 8.17, the Product column has a drop down arrow. This is because of the combo box that we created in FrmOrderDetail. Here you can select a product from the Product table. The drop down arrow will only appear when you click inside the Product box. If you need to change the width of any column, bring the mouse pointer to the separating vertical line between the two labels. When the pointer becomes a two headed arrow, drag the pointer in the required direction to get the required results.

- Close the form and save the changes to the design of the form

Creating Payment Subform

We want to create a Payment subform which will be a part of the main Order form. This form will be based on a query called QryPayment specifically created for this form. This subform and its underlying query will be used to enter method of payment information for customer's order.

Let us look at the relationship between the three tables as shown in figure 8.18. QryPayment must include OrderId from Invoice table so that the subform can later be linked to the main form (FrmOrder). To add method of payment information into PaymentMethod table, we need PymntMethodId from Invoice table so that the Invoice table can be linked to PaymentMethod table. We also need InvoiceId from Invoice table so that an invoice number can be assigned to a specific order and to its method of payment.

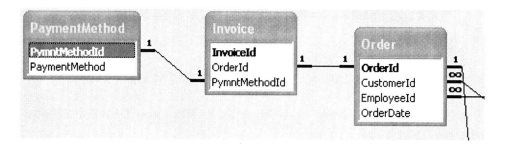

Figure 8.18

- In the database window select **Queries**, click the **New** button
- Double click **Design View**. This will bring the **Show Table** window

- Add the **Invoice** table and **PaymentMethod** table to the query window and then click **Close**
- From the **Invoice** table, add InvoiceId, OrderId and PymntMethodId to the QBE grid
- From **PaymentMethod** table, add PaymentMethod to the QBE grid as shown in figure 8.19

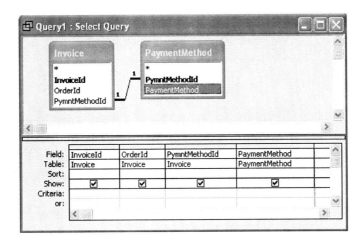

Figure 8.19

- Close the query and save it as **QryPayment**

Next we are going to create a form based on this query

- In the Database Window select **Forms** and click **New**
- In the New Form window select **AutoForm: Columnar**
- Select **QryPayment** from the drop down list and click **OK**. You will see a screen as shown in figure 8.20

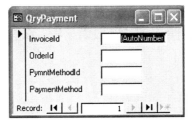

Figure 8.20

- Close the form and save it as **FrmPayment**
- In the **Forms** window click **FrmPayment** and then click **Design**. You will get a screen as shown in figure 8.21. If the window is not big enough, drag the outer borders of the window so that you can see all the fields in the window

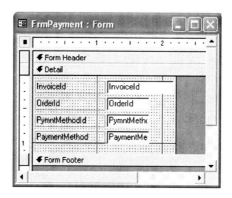

Figure 8.21

- Delete the **label** and **text box** for **OrderId**. We need OrderId in the query so that we can link this form with main order form but we do not need it in the form
- Delete the **label** and **text box** for **PymntMethodId**. We need **PymntMethodId** in the query so that we can link table **Invoice** with table **PaymentMethod** but we do not need it in the form
- Delete the **label** and **text box** for **PaymentMethod**. We need **PaymentMethod** on this form but it would be better if we introduce **Option group** for PaymentMethod

An Option group gives an employee specific choices and then entering the proper value for the selected choice into the underlying table. This makes an Option group entry quick and accurate.

- Right click anywhere in the empty space in **Detail** pane and select **Toolbox**
- Make sure that the **Control Wizard** button is depressed in Toolbox as shown in figure 8.22

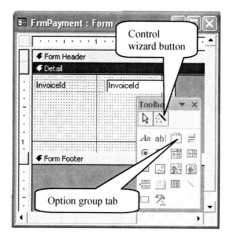

Figure 8.22

- Click the **Option group** tab and then click in the empty space under the **InvoiceId** where we want the Option group to appear. This will start the Option group wizard

- A message "**What label do you want for each option**" will appear
- Type **Cash** and then press Tab
- Type **Credit Card** and then press Tab
- Type **Debit Card** and then click **Next**
- This will bring the screen "**Do you want one option to be the default choice?**"
- Select **No, I don't want a default** and then click **Next**
- In this step Access assigns values of **1**, **2** and **3** to your labeled buttons. These values are fine and click **Next**
- In this step select **Store the value in this field** and then select **PaymentMethod** from the drop down list. Click **Next**
- In this step you are given the choice of selecting the format for the option group. Leave the default format which is **Option buttons** and style **Etched**. Click **Next**
- This brings the screen "**What caption do you want for the option group**". Type **Payment Method** in caption box and click **Finish**
- Close the **Toolbox** if it is still open

Your option group should look as shown in figure 8.23

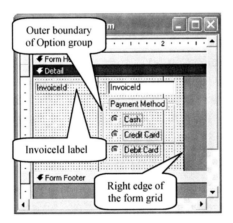

Figure 8.23

- Click inside the **InvoiceId label**. Decrease the size of the **InvoiceId label** box by dragging its right handle towards left so that **InvoiceId** can fit inside the box as shown in figure 8.24

Figure 8.24

- Click inside the **InvoiceId text box**. Drag the left handle for **InvoiceId text box** towards **InvoiceId label** until there is enough space between the label and the text box as shown in figure 8.24
- Drag the right handle for **InvoiceId text box** towards left so that **InvoiceId** can fit inside the box as shown in figure 8.24
- Click the outer boundary of Payment Method **Option group**. This will select everything in the option group. Move it towards left so that the right boundary of the option group aligns with the right boundary of **InvoiceId text box** as shown in figure 8.24
- Bring the mouse pointer to the right edge of the form grid. When the pointer becomes a two headed arrow, drag it toward left until all the controls can easily fit inside the form grid as shown in figure 8.24
- Close the form and save the changes to the design of the form

Adding a subform into a form

So far we created the main form and the two subforms. Now we can go ahead by adding the two subforms into the main form one by one. As we said before that to link a subform to a main form, you need a linking field that is shared by both forms.

Order table share a common OrderId field with OrderDetail table. This sharing enables FrmOrderDetail to display items for an order associated with the OrderId in FrmOrder. Therefore, we link FrmOrderDetail to FrmOrder through OrderId.

Order table also shares a common OrderId field with Invoice table. This sharing enables FrmPayment to display method of payment information in FrmOrder for an order associated with that specific OrderId. Therefore, we link FrmPayment to FrmOrder through OrderId.

- In the **Forms** window click **FrmOrder** and then click **Design**
- Move **FrmOrder** window towards right so that FrmOrder and the database window are side by side as shown in figure 8.25

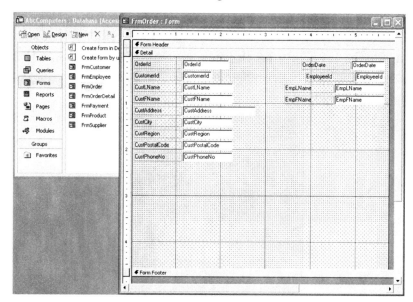

Figure 8.25

- Drag **FrmOrderDetail** from the database window and drop it in the empty space below the customer's details in **FrmOrder** window as shown in figure 8.26
- Click on the outer boundary of **QryOrderDetail** and this will highlight the outer boundary
- Bring the mouse pointer over the boundary and when it changes to a hand

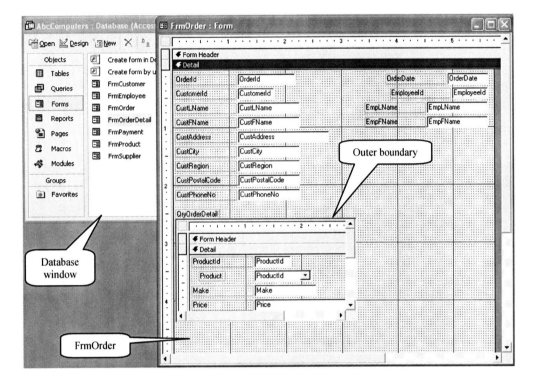

Figure 8.26

- Right click here and select **Properties**. Under **Data** tab you will see the screen shown in figure 8.27

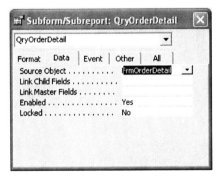

Figure 8.27

- Click in the **Link Child Fields** box and this will bring the build button (the small button with the three dots that appears to the right of the Link Child Fields box)

- Click the **Build button** and the **Subform Field Linker** dialog box appears as shown in figure 8.28

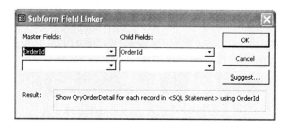

Figure 8.28

- Select **OrderId** for **Master Fields**
- Select **OrderId** for **Child Fields** and click **OK**

The linking fields appear in the properties dialog box as shown in figure 8.29. Now the main form and the subform are linked by OrderId

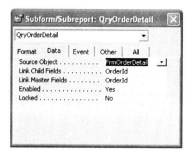

Figure 8.29

- Close the **Subform/Subreport** window
- Open **FrmOrder** in **Datasheet** view by clicking **Datasheet tab** ⊞ ▾ on the Toolbar and you will see the screen shown in figure 8.30

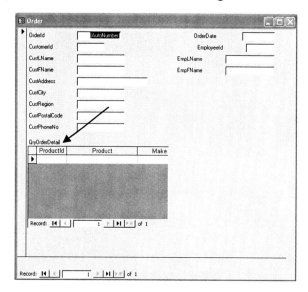

Figure 8.30

We can not see all the fields in QryOrderDetail. We have to change the subform so that all the fields are visible.

- Open **FrmOrder** in **Design** view by clicking 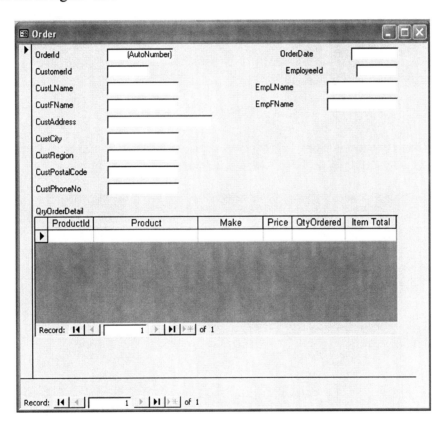 Design on the Toolbar
- Click on the outer boundary of **QryOrderDetail** to select it
- Bring the mouse pointer to the right border of the subform where the pointer becomes a two headed arrow (over the black dot)
- Drag the border towards right
- Click the **Datasheet** view on the Toolbar and check if you can see all the fields in **QryOrderDetail**
- Switch back to **Design** view by clicking Design on the Toolbar. Adjust the form size in **Design** view until you can see all the fields in the **Datasheet** view as shown in figure 8.31

Figure 8.31

- Close the form and save the changes to the design of the form

Next we want to add FrmPayment to FrmOrder.

- In the database window, click **Forms** if not selected
- Open **FrmOrder** in design view
- Move **FrmOrder** window towards right so that **FrmOrder** and the database window are side by side as shown in figure 8.32

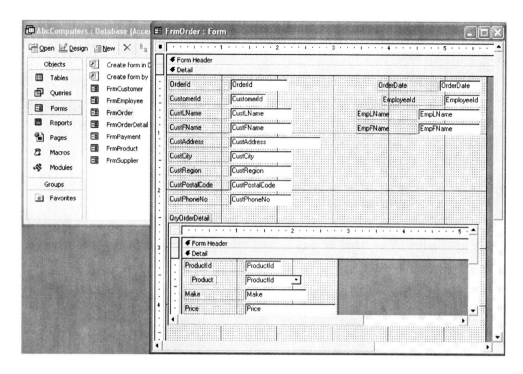

Figure 8.32

- Drag **FrmPayment** from database window and drop it in the empty space below the employee details in **FrmOrder** window as shown in figure 8.33

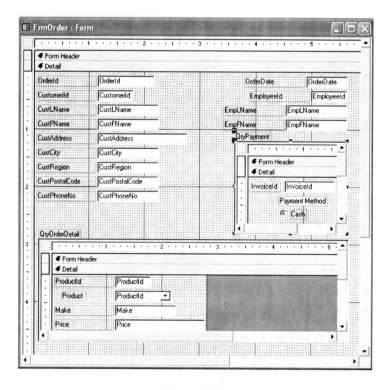

Figure 8.33

- Click on the outer boundary of **QryPayment** and this will highlight **QryPayment**
- Bring the mouse pointer over the boundary and when it changes to a hand
- Right click here and select **Properties**. Under **Data** tab you will see the screen shown in figure 8.34

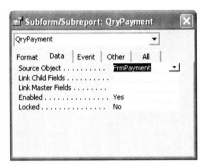

Figure 8.34

- Click in the **Link Child Fields** box and this will bring the build button (the small button with the three dots that appears to the right of the Link Child Fields box)
- Click the **Build button** and the **Subform Field Linker** dialog box appears as shown in figure 8.35

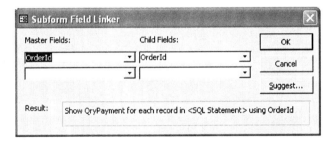

Figure 8.35

- Select **OrderId** in **Master Fields**
- Select **OrderId** in **Child Fields** and click **OK**

The linking fields appear in the properties dialog box. Now the main form and the subform are linked by OrderId as shown in figure 8.36

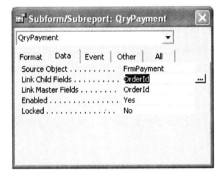

Figure 8.36

- Close the **Subform/Subreport** window
- Switch to **Datasheet** view by clicking the datasheet tab on the Toolbar and you will see the screen shown in figure 8.37

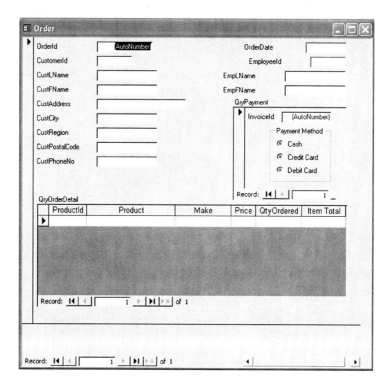

Figure 8.37

- Close the form and save the changes to the design of the form

Finishing the main form
Currently FrmOrder can not do all the functions that we want it to do. They are

- When an employee is taking an order, there should be a drop down list where the employee can select their name from the Employee table and be associated with that order. You need a combo box for this option to be available
- In case of an existing customer, the employee should be able to select the name of the customer from the Customer table through a drop down list. You need a combo box for this option to be available
- When an employee is taking an order for a new customer, there should be a command button that could bring the New Customer form to add the new customer

Let us start creating a combo box that can list all the employees in the Employee table

- In database window, Click **Forms**
- Open **FrmOrder** in design view as shown in figure 8.38

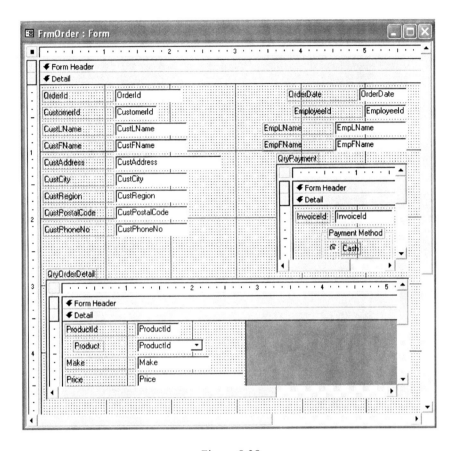

Figure 8.38

- Delete **EmployeeId** label and text box
- Delete **EmpLName** label and text box
- Delete **EmpFName** label and text box
- Right click anywhere in the empty space in **Detail** pane and select **Toolbox**
- Click the **Combo box** tab in the Toolbox and then click in the empty space under **OrderDate**. This will start the Combo box wizard
- Select "**I want the combo box to look up the values in a table or query**" and click **Next**
- Select **Table: Employee** and click **Next**
- Add **EmpFName** and **EmpLName** into the **Selected Fields** as shown in figure 8.39

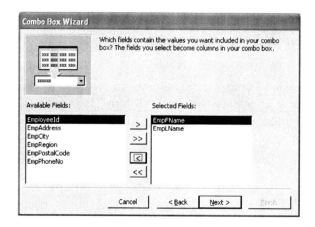

Figure 8.39

- Click **Next** and you will get the screen shown in figure 8.40

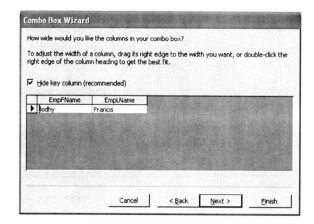

Figure 8.40

- Adjust the two columns labels if they are not wide enough for the names to fit in
- Leave the **Hide Key column** checked
- Click **Next** and you will get a screen as shown in figure 8.41

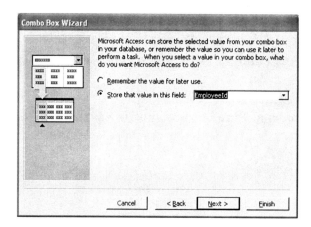

Figure 8.41

- Click **Store that value in this field:** Select **EmployeeId** from the drop down list
- Click **Next** and you will get a screen as shown in figure 8.42

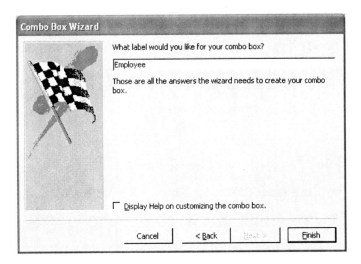

Figure 8.42

- Name the combo box label as **Employee** and click **Finish**
- Switch to **Datasheet** View and you will see a screen as shown in figure 8.43
- Click the Employee drop down arrow and you will see a list of employees
- Select the available employee Jodhy Francis from the list. We added this employee in chapter 6 when we created **FrmEmployee**

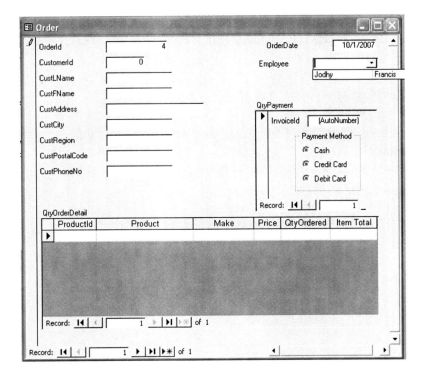

Figure 8.43

You will notice that once you select an employee, it only shows the first name of an employee instead of the full name in the box. To fix this problem, we take the following steps

- Close **FrmOrder**. You will get a screen as shown in figure 8.44

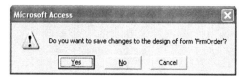

Figure 8.44

- Click **Yes**. You will get a screen as shown in figure 8.45

Figure 8.45

- Click **Ok**. You will get a screen as shown in figure 8.46

Figure 8.46

- Click **Yes** and the window will close
- Open **FrmOrder** in **Design** view.
- Right click on **EmployeeId** text box (within the combo box) and select **Properties**
- Select the **All** tab and then click in **Row Source**. This will bring the **Build button** on the right side as shown in figure 8.47

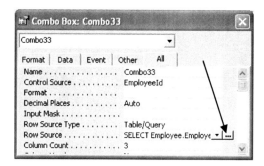

Figure 8.47

- Click on the **Build button** and this will bring the screen in figure 8.48

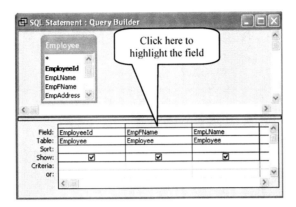

Figure 8.48

- Click in the grey box on the top of **EmpFName**, this will highlight **EmpFName** field. Delete this field
- Click in the grey box on the top of **EmpLName**, this will highlight **EmpLName** field. Delete this field
- In the empty field next to EmployeeId field, type

Expr1: [Employee].[EmpFName] & " " & [Employee].[EmpLName]

You will get the screen shown in figure 8.49

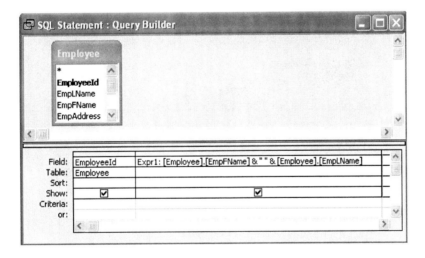

Figure 8.49

- Close the **Query Builder** window and you will get a screen as shown in figure 8.50

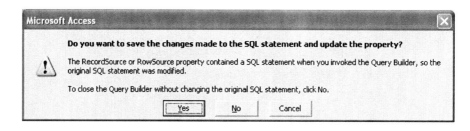

Figure 8.50

- Click **Yes**. This will bring you back to **Combo Box** window
- Close the **Combo Box** window
- Switch to **Datasheet** View
- Click the drop down list for **Employee** and select Jodhy Francis from the list. This time you can see Jodhy Francis's full name in Employee box once selected
- Close **FrmOrder** and you will get a screen as shown in figure 8.51

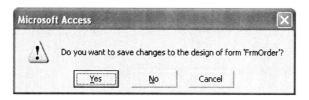

Figure 8.51

- Click **Yes**. This will bring another screen as shown in figure 8.52

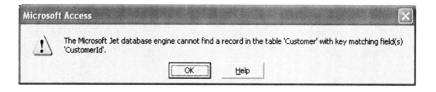

Figure 8.52

- Click **Ok**. This will bring another screen as shown in figure 8.53

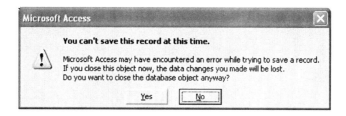

Figure 8.53

- Click **Yes**. This will bring you back to the database window.

Next we want to create a combo box that can list the customers in Customer table

- Open **FrmOrder** in **Design** view
- Delete **CustLName** label and text box
- Delete **CustFName** label and text box
- Right click anywhere in the empty space in **Detail** pane and select **Toolbox**
- Click the **Combo box** tab and then click in the empty space under **CustomerId**. This will start the Combo box wizard
- Select "**I want the combo box to look up the values in a table or query**" and click **Next**
- Select **Table: Customer** and click **Next**
- Add **CustFName** and **CustLName** into the **Selected Fields** and click **Next**
- Adjust the two columns labels so that they are wide enough for the names to fit in. Leave the **Hide Key column** checked and click **Next**
- Select **Store that value in this field:** Select **CustomerId** from the dropdown window and then click **Next**
- Name the combo box label as **Customer** and click **Finish**
- Switch to **Datasheet** View and you will get a screen as shown in figure 8.54

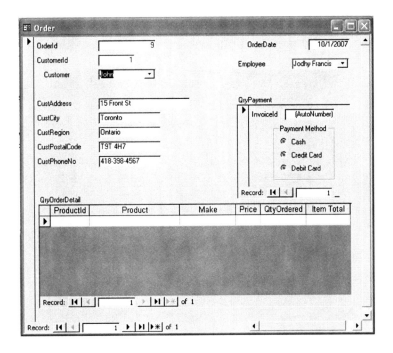

Figure 8.54

- Click the **Employee** drop down list and select one of the employee from the list
- Click the **Customer** drop down list and select one customer (John Doe) from the list. We added this customer in chapter 6 when we created FrmCustomer

As you can see in figure 8.54, you can select John Doe from the Customer table. When you select the customer, it only shows John's first name on the screen. To fix this problem, we take the following steps

- Open **FrmOrder** in **Design** view by clicking 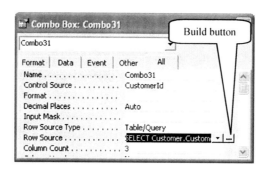 Design on the Toolbar
- Right click on **CustomerId** text box (within the combo box) and select **Properties**. You will get a screen as shown in figure 8.55

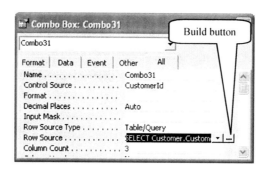

Figure 8.55

- Select **All** tab and then Click in **Row Source**. This will bring the **Build button** on the right side as shown in figure 8.55
- Click on the **Build button** and this will bring the screen in figure 8.56

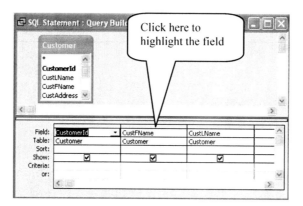

Figure 8.56

- Click in the grey box on the top of **CustFName**, this will highlight CustFName field. Delete this field
- Click in the grey box on the top of **CustLName**, this will highlight CustLName field. Delete this field
- In the empty field next to CustomerId field, type

Expr1: [Customer].[CustFName] & " " & [Customer].[CustLName]

You will get a screen as shown in figure 8.57

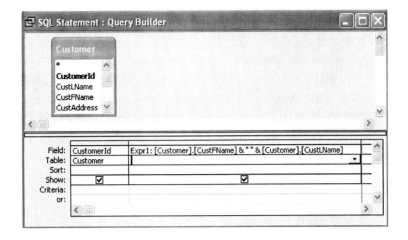

Figure 8.57

- Close the **Query Builder** window and you will get the screen in figure 8.58

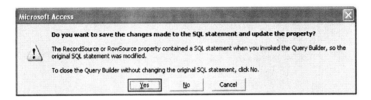

Figure 8.58

- Click **Yes**. This will bring you back to the Combo Box window
- Close the **Combo Box** window
- Switch to **Datasheet** View. You will get a screen as shown in figure 8.59

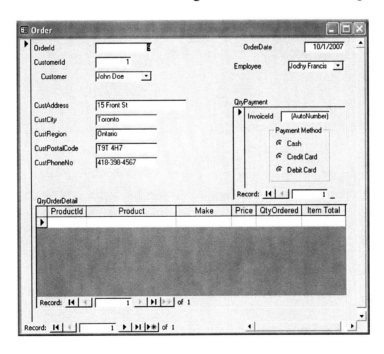

Figure 8.59

As you can see, the problem has been resolved. Now you can see the Customer's full name in Customer box.

Consider you are taking an order from a customer. You found that the customer is not in the list. Now you need some way of adding the customer to the database. In Chapter 6, we created a form called FrmCustomer to add customers. Now you need that form to add a new customer in to the database. To start FrmCustomer within FrmOrder, we need the Command button option available in Microsoft Access. We will place the Command button next to OrderId in FrmOrder.

Let us start creating the Command button

- Open **FrmOrder** in **Design** view
- Right click anywhere in the empty space and select **Toolbox**
- Click the **Command button** in the Tool box to select it as shown in figure 8.60

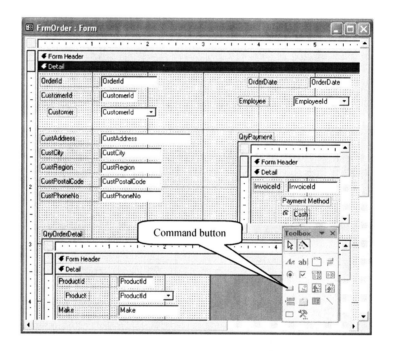

Figure 8.60

- We want the Command button next to OrderId. Click to the right of **OrderId**. This will start the Command button wizard as shown in figure 8.61

163

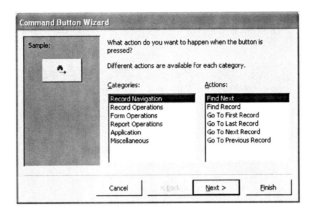

Figure 8.61

- In **Categories** select **Form Operations**
- In **Actions** select **Open Form**
- Click **Next** and you will get a screen as shown in figure 8.62. Select **FrmCustomer**

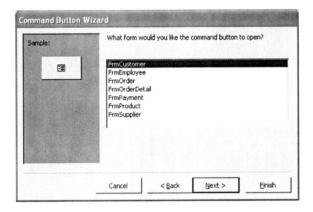

Figure 8.62

- Click **Next** and you will get a screen as shown in figure 8.63. Select "**Open the form and show all the records**"

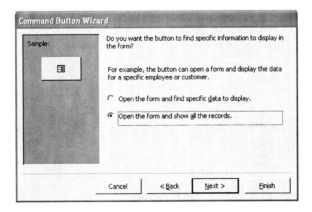

Figure 8.63

- Click **Next** and you will get a screen as shown in figure 8.64. Select **Text: Open Form**

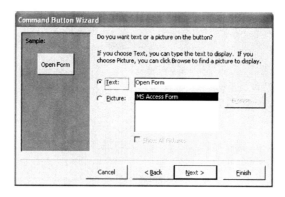

Figure 8.64

- Click **Next** and you will get a screen as shown in figure 8.65. Type **NewCustomer**

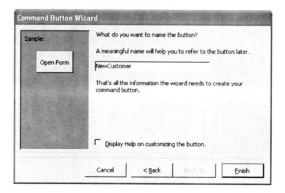

Figure 8.65

- Click **Finish**. You will get a screen as shown in figure 8.66

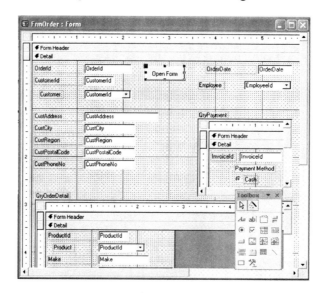

Figure 8.66

The new Command button is named as **Open Form** as shown in the figure 8.66. We want to change this name to **New Customer**

- Right Click **Open Form** and select **Properties**
- Select the **All** tab. This will bring the screen in figure 8.67

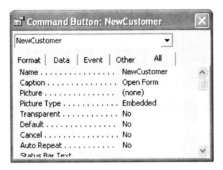

Figure 8.67

- Click in **Caption** box and delete the name **Open Form**. We want to name the Command button as **New Customer**
- Type **New Customer** and close the window
- Drag the right border of the **Command button** towards right so that you can see the whole name for the Command button
- Switch to **Datasheet** view and **FrmOrder** should look as shown in figure 8.68

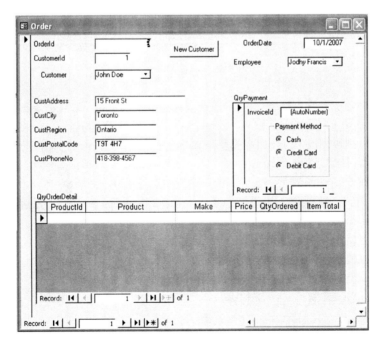

Figure 8.68

- Click on **New Customer** command button. This will bring **FrmCustomer**
- Close **FrmCustomer** window

- Close **FrmOrder** window and save changes to the design of the form

Entering an Order into the Database
Let us enter a dummy Order in to the database.

- In the database window, select **Forms**
- Double click **FrmOrder** and you will get a screen as shown in figure 8.69

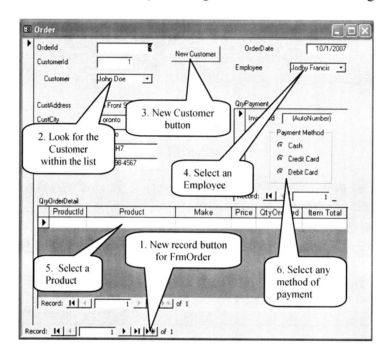

Figure 8.69

- Click the **New record** button for **FrmOrder** and you will get a blank order form
- We have a customer Jane Doe. You look for her in **Customer** drop down list but you can not see her in the list. This means that she is not in the database and you have to add her to the database
- Click **New Customer** button. This will bring **FrmCustomer**
- Click the **New record** button (an arrow head next to a star) within **FrmCustomer**. Type the following
- In **CustLName**, type Doe
- Tab out to **CustFName**, type Jane
- Tab out to **CustAddress**, type 10 Kingston Ave
- Tab out to **CustCity**, type Kingston
- Tab out to **CustRegion**, type Ontario
- Tab out to **CustPostalCode**, type M6K 3J3
- Tab out to **CustPhoneNo**, type 905-278-1234
- Close **FrmCustomer** window
- Now you click the **Customer** drop down list and you still can not see the new customer in the list

Important: Press the **F9** key. Pressing the F9 key tells Microsoft Access to query the Customer table for current data. Once the query has completed, the new record will appear in Customer drop down list.

- Select Jane Doe in **Customer** drop down list
- Select Jodhy Francis as the **Employee** taking the order from the drop down list. Currently, Jodhy is the only employee on the list. You can add more employees to the list by using **FrmEmployee** in Forms window
- Click inside the **Product** box and then select a product. Type the quantity that the customer ordered in **QtyOrdered** box. The default **QtyOrdered** is 1. For any additional products, add each product one by one in the following lines

For any new product that is not on the list, you have to go to **FrmProduct** and add it over there into the database and then you can select it over here.

- Select **Cash** as method of payment for this order under **Payment Method** as shown in figure 8.70

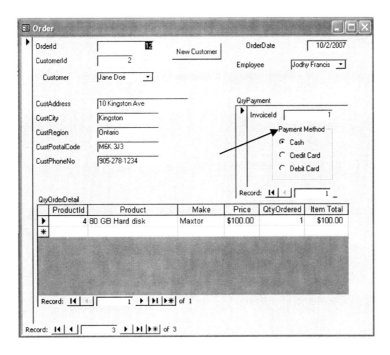

Figure 8.70

When you click on an option in Payment Method, an **InvoiceId** is assigned to that Order and its associated method of payment.

- This order is complete. To create another order, click the **New record** button for **FrmOrder** and repeat all the previous steps again. Remember to enter the order in this order otherwise you may get an error
- Once you are done. Close **FrmOrder** window

Adding a Calculated Control to a Form

We want the Order form to show the total for an order. Order total is the sum of **Item Total** in FrmOderDetail. Let us create an unbound text box in FrmOrderDetail footer to sum the values in **Item Total** text boxes.

- In the database window, select **Forms**
- Open **FrmOrderDetail** in **Design** view
- Maximize the **FrmOrderDetail** window.
- Bring the mouse pointer to the left bottom border of **Form Footer** bar. When the pointer becomes a two headed arrow, drag it down to make enough space for a new **Text box** as shown in figure 8.71
- Right click anywhere in the empty space in the grid and select **Toolbox**
- Click the **Text Box** button in the **Toolbox**
- Click in the newly created space in form footer. A new **Text box** will appear in the form footer as shown in figure 8.71
- Click anywhere in the empty space to deselect the **Text box** controls
- Click only the **Label** for the text box and press **Delete**
- Click twice inside the **Text box** (not a double click)
- Inside the **Text box**, type =sum([Item Total]) and then press Enter

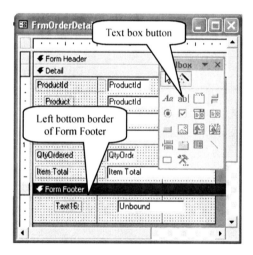

Figure 8.71

- Right click the **Text box** and select **Properties**
- On the **All** tab, in the **Name** box, delete what is there and type **OrderTotal**. Your **Properties** window should look as shown in figure 8.72.
- Close the **Properties** window

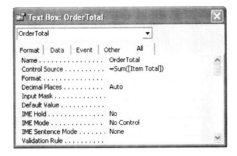

Figure 8.72

- Close **FrmOrderDetail** window and save changes to the design of the form

You will not be able to see the results of your calculated control because the subform footer is hidden. We will create a text box in the main Order form that displays the value from the text box in **FrmOrderDetail** footer.

- Open **FrmOrder** in **Design** view
- Maximize the **FrmOrder** window
- Bring the mouse pointer to the top border of **Form Footer** bar, when the pointer becomes a two headed arrow, drag it down to make enough room for a Text Box as shown in figure 8.73
- Right click in the empty space in the grid and select **Toolbox**
- Click the **Text Box** button in the **Toolbox**
- Click in the right bottom corner of **FrmOrder** and this will create a **Text box** in this space as shown in figure 8.73

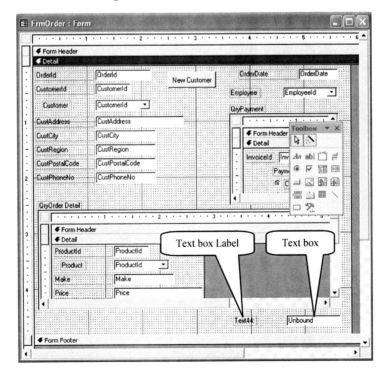

Figure 8.73

- Click inside the **Label** for the **Text Box** and type **Order Total**
- Right click the **Text box** and select **Properties**
- Click the **All** tab. In the **Name** box type **MainTotal**
- In the **Control Source** box type
  =[QryOrderDetail].[Form]![OrderTotal]
- In the **Format** box click the down arrow and then select **Currency**. Your **Properties** screen should look as shown in figure 8.74

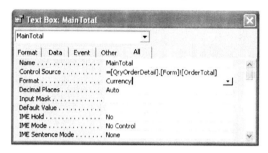

Figure 8.74

- Close the **Properties** window
- Switch to **Datasheet** view
- Enter a new order. You will get an **Order Total** of $700.00 (for two 80 GB Hard disks and one 19 inch LCD monitor) as shown in figure 8.75.

If you do not see the right amount, then press **F9** key. This will run the query again so that you can see the latest information.

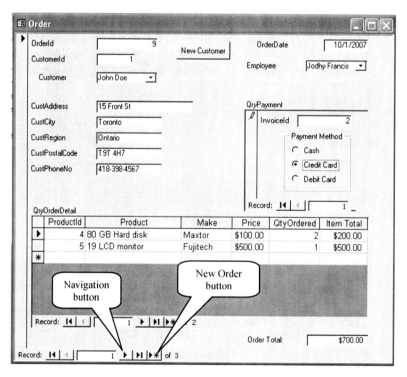

Figure 8.75

- Close **FrmOrder** and save changes to the design of the form

Now this is a good time to enter a few new products to the database using **FrmProduct**. Add a few new employees to the database using **FrmEmployee**. Enter a few dummy orders to the database so that you have some data for the reports to work with in the next chapter. Do not forget to press the new order button each time you enter a new order.

Tweaking FrmOrder

If you look at FrmOrder in figure 8.75, you would notice that you can change the data in many places. As an example, currently the price of an 80 GB Hard disk is $100.00. If you want to change the price to $150.00 in this form, you can make the change without any problem. We do not want anybody being able to change the price in this form. To solve this problem, we restrict the entry of data to some specific places in the form. There are navigation buttons in **QryPayment** and **QryOrderDetail** subforms. We do not want these buttons there too. The subform names **QryPayment** and **QryOrderDetail** are also not very intuitive.

- Open **FrmOrder** in **Design** view as shown in figure 8.76

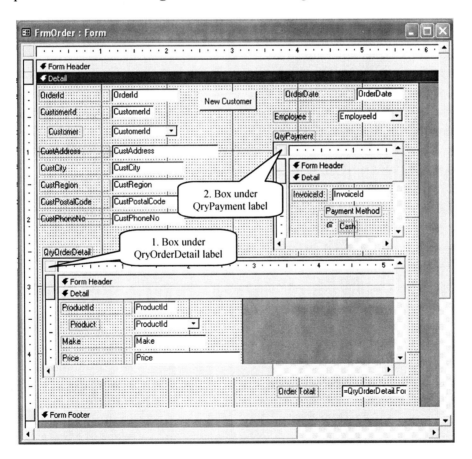

Figure 8.76

- Right click **OrderDate** Text box in **FrmOrder** and select **Properties**

172

- Click the **Data** tab
- Click in the **Locked** box, click the down arrow and then select **Yes**
- Close the **Properties** window

Locking the control prevents the user from making changes to the data.

- In **QryOrderDetail** subform, right click **Price** Text box
- Select **Properties** and click the **Data** tab
- Click in the **Locked** box, click the down arrow and then select **Yes**
- Close the **Properties** window
- Repeat the same procedure for **ProductId** and **Make** text boxes in **QryOrderDetail** subform
- Once you are done, switch to **Datasheet** view and you should not be able to change the data in the selected fields

Next we want to remove the navigation buttons for **QryOrderDetail** and **QryPayment** subforms

- Switch back to **Design** view
- Click twice (no double click) inside the box under **QryOrderDetail** label as shown in figure 8.76. Once selected, right click on it and select **Properties**
- Click the **All** tab
- Click in the **Navigation buttons** box, click the down arrow and then select **No**
- Close the **Properties** window
- Scroll down in **QryOrderDetail** subform until you find **QtyOrdered**
- Right click on **QtyOrdered** Label and select **Properties**
- Click the **All** tab
- Click in the **Caption** box and delete what is there. Type **Quantity**
- Close the **Properties** window
- Right click on **QryOrderDetail** label and select **Properties**
- Click the **All** tab
- Click in the **Caption** box and delete what is there. Type **Order Detail**
- Close the **Properties** window

- Click twice (no double click) inside the box under **QryPayment** label as shown in figure 8.76. Once selected, right click on it and select **Properties**
- Click the **All** tab,
- Click in the **Navigation buttons** box, click the down arrow and then select **No**
- Close the **Properties** window
- Right click on **QryPayment** label and select **Properties**
- Click the **All** tab
- Click in the **Caption** box and delete what is there. Type **Payment**
- Close the **Properties** window

- Switch to **Datasheet** view and you should see the screen in figure 8.77

You would notice that the label for **QryOrderDetail** has changed to **Order Detail**. The navigation buttons in **Order Detail** are gone. You would also notice that the label for **QryPayment** has changed to **Payment**. The navigation buttons in **Payment** are not there any more. You also can not change the data for the fields that you have locked.

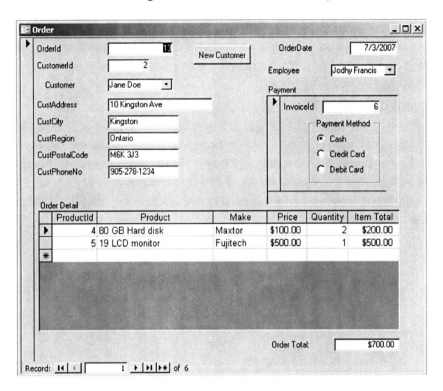

Figure 8.77

- Close **FrmOrder** and save changes to the design of the Form

As you can see, FrmOrder is working fine and can do all the functions you expect it to do. Now the next question is "How do we put all the information in FrmOrder together so that we can print an invoice?" We are going to address this issue in the next chapter.

Chapter 9

Reports

Creating a report is similar to creating a form. You can create one quickly by using the default autoreport or you can use the report wizard to produce results more tailored to your needs. If a specialized report is required, you can customize reports using many of the same techniques we used for forms.

Creating AutoReports

Autoreports do not offer much choice but are very fast. You can create a report on either a table or a query. It is a good idea to base reports on queries because the report will load faster and will be easier to build as only the query fields will be used in the report. You can create a Columnar or a Tabular report. We will create both

- In the database window, select **Reports** and click **New**. You will get a screen as shown in figure 9.1

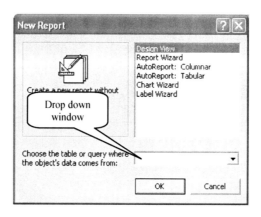

Figure 9.1

- Select **AutoReport: Columnar**
- Select **QryListSuppliers** in the drop down window and click **Ok**

This will get you a Columnar report as shown in figure 9.2.

- Close the report. You will be asked "**Do you want to save changes to the design of the report 'Report1'**"
- Click **Yes** and give it a name "**RptClmnListSuppliers**"
- Click **Ok** and the report will be created

Next time you want to run the report, you just double click the report and you will get a Columnar AutoReport for the list of suppliers.

Next we will create a Tabular AutoReport.

- In the database window, select **Reports** and click **New**
- Select **AutoReport: Tabular**
- Select **QryListSuppliers** in the drop down window and click **Ok**

This will get you a Tabular report as shown in figure 9.3.

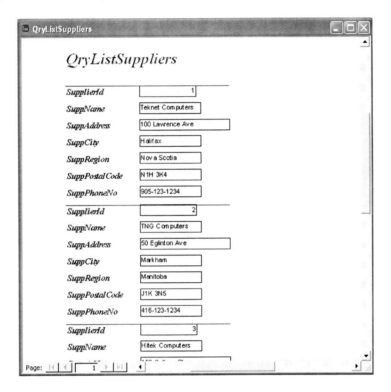

Figure 9.2

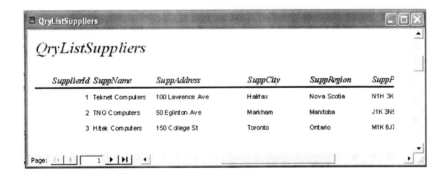

Figure 9.3

- Close the report. You will be asked "**Do you want to save changes to the design of the report 'Report1'**"
- Click **Yes** and give it a name "**RptTblrListSuppliers**"
- Click **Ok** and the report will be created

Using the Report Wizard

The advantage of using the report wizard is that it asks you for input when it creates your report. This means that you have more choices than you do with an autoreport and the finished report requires less tweaking.

- In the database window, select **Reports** and click **New**
- Select **Report Wizard**
- Select **QryListSuppliers** in the bottom list box and click **Ok**

This will bring the screen in figure 9.4. As you can see in the figure, you are given the choice of what fields to add to the report.

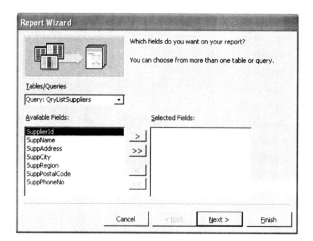

Figure 9.4

- Add all the fields to the **Selected Fields** list by clicking the right double arrow
- Click **Next**. The second wizard step appears as shown in figure 9.5

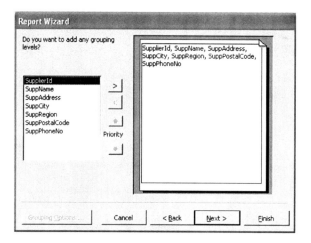

Figure 9.5

- We do not want any **grouping levels**. Click **Next**

177

- This step gives you the choice of a **sort order** for your records as shown in figure 9.6. We are not interested in any sort order. Click **Next**.

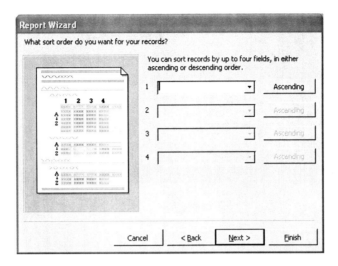

Figure 9.6

- This step gives you the choice of a **lay out** for your report as shown in figure 9.7. The default lay out (tabular and portrait) is fine for this report. Click **Next**

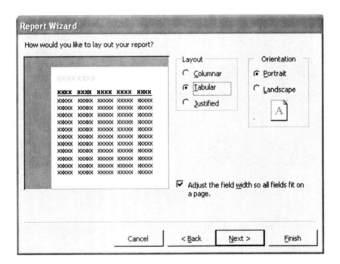

Figure 9.7

- This step gives you the choice of **six styles** for your report as shown in figure 9.8. Leave the default (Corporate) style. Click **Next**

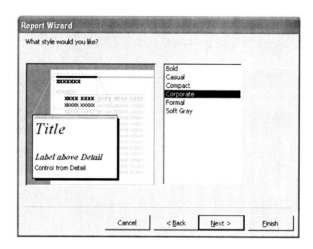

Figure 9.8

- The last wizard step appears as shown in figure 9.9. Give the report a name of **RptWizListSuppliers**

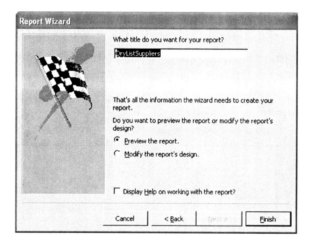

Figure 9.9

- Click **Finish**. This will create the report as shown in figure 9.10
- Close the report window

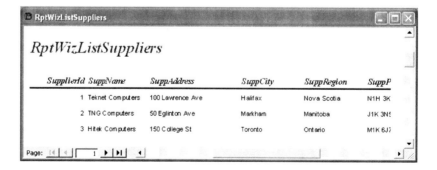

Figure 9.10

Creating an Invoice for a Customer

To create an invoice, we need all the information from Order form. To get all the information from FrmOrder, we need a query that can combine all the three queries that make up FrmOrder i.e. QryOrder, QryOrderDetail and QryPayment. As the result of each query is a table, we join all the three resulting tables by OrderId. Then we add all the required fields from the three tables to the QBE grid.

Let us start creating this query as following

- In the database window, select **Queries** and click **New**. This will bring a window as shown in figure 9.11

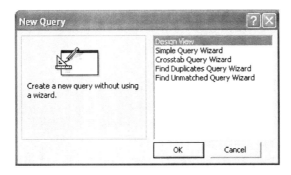

Figure 9.11

- Double click **Design View**. This will bring a **Show table** window on the top of QBE grid as shown in figure 9.12

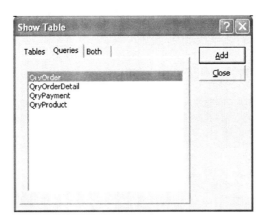

Figure 9.12

- In **Show Table** window, Click on **Queries** tab
- Add **QryOrderDetail**, **QryOrder** and **QryPayment** to the QBE grid
- Close the **Show table** window. You will get a screen as shown in figure 9.13

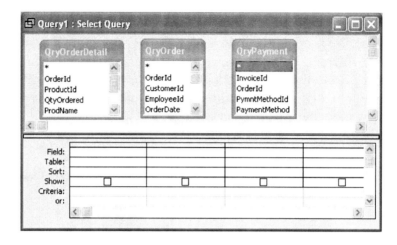

Figure 9.13

- Drag **OrderId** from table **QryOrderDetail** to **OrderId** in **QryOrder**. This will make the two tables joined by **OrderId**
- Drag **OrderId** from table **QryOrder** to **OrderId** in table **QryPayment**. This will make the two tables joined by **OrderId**
- From table **QryOrder** add OrderId, CustomerId, EmployeeId, OrderDate, CustLName, CustFName, CustAddress, CustCity, CustRegion, CustPostalCode, CustPhoneNo, EmpLName and EmpFName to the QBE grid by double clicking each field
- From table **QryOrderDetail** add ProductId, QtyOrdered, ProdName, Make, Price and Item Total to the QBE grid by double clicking each field
- From table **QryPayment** add InvoiceId, PymntMethodId and PaymentMethod to the QBE grid by double clicking each field

You will get a screen as shown in figure 9.14

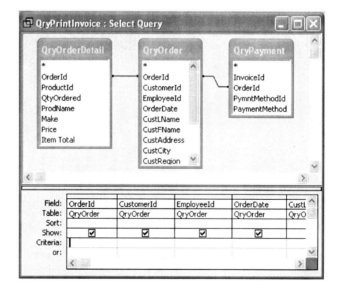

Figure 9.14

- Close the query window and you will get a screen as shown in figure 9.15

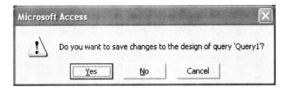

Figure 9.15

- Click **Yes**. This will bring the **Save As** window as shown in figure 9.16

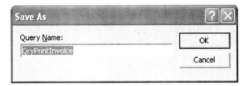

Figure 9.16

- Type **QryPrintInvoice** and click **Ok**. This will save the query

Next we want the information gathered in **QryPrintInvoice** query to be printed as an invoice. To print something in Access, you need to use the print report function.

Creating Print Invoice report

We are going to create a report in the form of an invoice for a customer. The invoice will be printed on a normal A4 paper.

Let us create a Tabular AutoReport and then customize it to suit our needs.

- In database window, select **Reports** and click **New**
- Select **AutoReport: Tabular**
- Select **QryPrintInvoice** in the bottom list box and click **Ok**

This will create a Tabular report as shown in figure 9.17. This report does not look much like an invoice. We will work on it to make it look like an invoice.

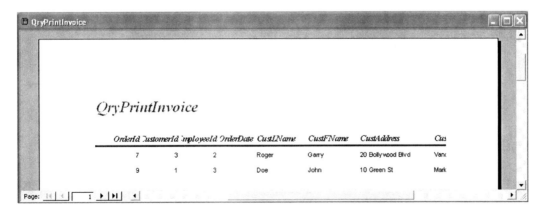

Figure 9.17

- Close the report. This will bring the screen in figure 9.18

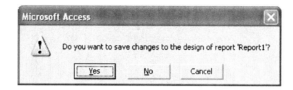

Figure 9.18

- Click **Yes** and this will bring the screen in figure 9.19

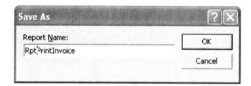

Figure 9.19

- Type **RptPrintInvoice** and click **Ok**
- While still in the **Reports** window, click the **RptPrintInvoice** to select it and then click **Design** to open the report in **Design** view as shown in figure 9.20

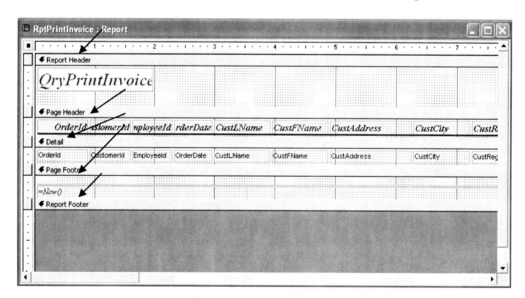

Figure 9.20

You will see five parts for the report in the Design view. They are as following

Report Header: This is the top part of the report. Controls in the Report Header appear only once at the beginning of the report.
Page Header: Controls in the Page Header appear at the top of every page. It is suitable for columns headings.

Detail: This is used for the data in the report.

Page Footer: Controls in the Page Footer appear at the bottom of every page. The wizard inserts the page number and the date in this part of the report.

Report Footer: This is the last part of the report. Controls in the Report Footer appear only once at the end of the report.

Consider you go to a store and buy a product. You get an invoice once you pay for that product. You would notice that the invoice has a Company name, address, phone number, Invoice number, Order date, Customer name, address, phone number, Employee name and Method of payment information. All this information appears once at the start of an Invoice. As all this information needs to appear once at the start of an invoice, therefore, we could put all this information in Report Header. Any invoice would also have product information. Product information is arranged in the form of columns. The columns are labeled as ProductId, Product, Make, Price, Quantity and Item Total. Under each column label there is the data for that column. As each column label appears once on the invoice, we could place the labels in page header. The data under each column label appears many times, therefore, we can place the text box for each column in detail pane.

Considering the above discussion, we will populate the different parts of the report according to the following plan

- Delete any unnecessary controls in the report
- Place all customer Controls (label and text box) in **Report Header** section because they appear once on the invoice
- Place Invoice and Payment controls (label and text box) in **Report Header** section as they appear once on the invoice
- Place Employee Controls (label and text box) in **Report Header** section because they appear once on the invoice
- Place all Product labels in **Page Header** so that it gives a name to a column
- Place all Product text boxes in **Detail** pane (under related product labels) so that we get a tabular structure

Let us start designing the report

- In the **Report Header** in figure 9.20, click in **QryPrintInvoice** box and then delete QryPrintInvoice using Backspace. Type **Invoice**
- Click anywhere in the empty space in the grid to get out of the box
- Click on the border of **Invoice** box. Once highlighted, drag the right border of the box towards left so that Invoice can fit in the box
- Click on the border of **Invoice** box if not selected. Once highlighted, click the **Italic** button I to deselect it
- Move the **Invoice** label to the centre of **Report Header** as shown in figure 9.21
- Delete **OrderId**, **CustomerId**, **EmployeeId** and **PymntMethodId** labels and text boxes one by one as we do not need this information on the Invoice. You can use the bottom scroll bar right and left to look for anything that you can not see on the screen

- Bring the mouse pointer to the top border of the **Page Header** bar where the pointer becomes a two headed arrow. Drag downward until there is enough space to fit all Customer controls in **Report Header** as shown in figure 9.21
- Move **Customer** related labels and text boxes from **Page Header** and **Detail** pane towards **Report Header** as shown in figure 9.21. Pay attention to the squares in the figure, this will make your life easier
- Move **InvoiceId** label and text box to the top right hand corner of **Report Header** as shown in figure 9.21
- Place **OrderDate** label and text box under **InvoiceId** in the **Report Header** as shown in figure 9.21
- Drag the left hand border of **OrderDate** label towards left so that the text can fit nicely with in the label as shown in figure 9.21
- Place **PaymentMethod** label and text box under **OrderDate** in the **Report Header** as shown in figure 9.21. Make the PaymentMethod controls the same size as shown in figure. You may have to scroll right to see these controls
- Place **EmpFName**, **EmpLName** labels and text boxes under **PaymentMethod** in the **Report Header** as shown in figure 9.21

Figure 9.21

- Delete **CustLName** label as we do not need this label
- Rename **CustFName** label to **Customer** as shown in figure 9.22
- Delete the **Cust** part from Customer labels only as shown in figure 9.22
- Delete **EmpLName** label as we do not need this label
- Rename **EmpFName** label to **Employee** as shown in figure 9.22
- Press the **Shift** key and then click each label in **Report Header** to select it

- Click the **Italic** button I to deselect it. This will make each label look upright as shown in figure 9.22
- Click in the empty space in the grid to deselect the highlighted labels in **Report Header**
- Press the **Shift** key and then click each text box in **Report Header** to select it
- Click the **Align Left** button to align the result of each text box towards left as shown in figure 9.22

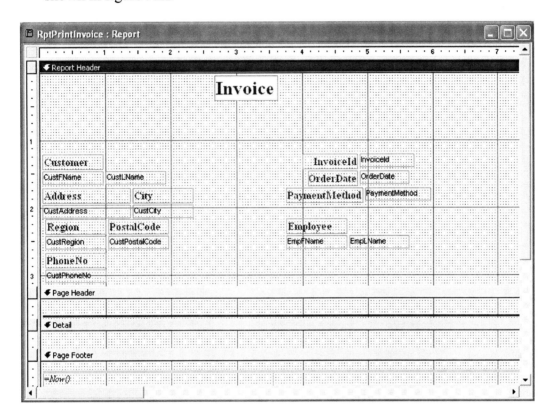

Figure 9.22

In figure 9.22, we do not see anything related to **Product**. Scroll towards right and you will see the rest of the controls.

- Move **ProductId** label in **Page Header** toward far left and place it above the **Blue line** in **Page Header** as shown in figure 9.23
- Move **ProductId** text box in **Detail** pane toward far left and place it in **Detail** pane under **ProductId** label in **Page Header** as shown in figure 9.23
- Move **ProdName, Make, Price, QtyOrdered** and **Item Total** labels towards left in **Page Header** and placing it next to each other as shown in figure 9.23. Make sure they are in this order and above the blue line
- Move **ProdName, Make, Price, QtyOrdered** and **Item Total** text boxes in **Detail** pane towards left and place it next to each other under there respective labels in **Page Header** as shown in figure 9.23

186

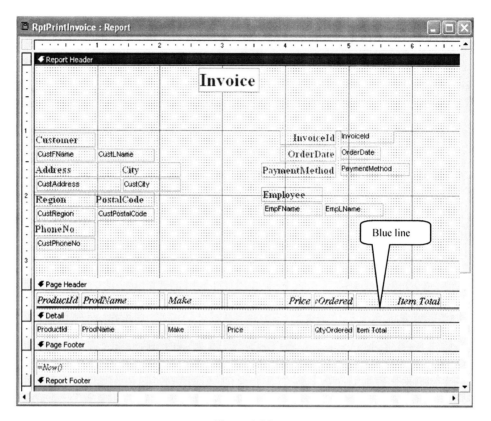

Figure 9.23

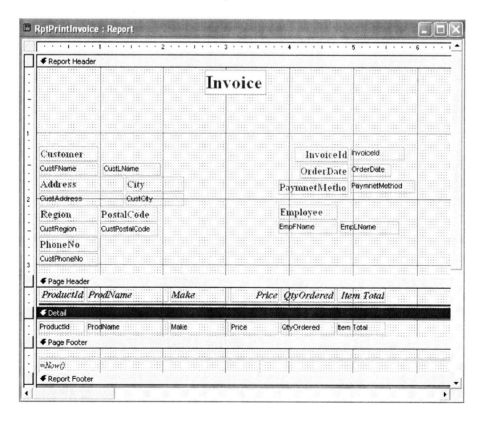

Figure 9.24

- Decrease the size of **Price** Label and Text box by dragging it towards left as shown in figure 9.24
- Move **QtyOrdered** Label and Text box towards left next to **Price** Label and Text box as shown in figure 9.24
- Increase the size of **QtyOrdered** Label and Text box towards right so that the text fit within the boxes as shown in figure 9.24
- Decrease the size of **Item Total** Label and Text box by dragging its right handle towards left and then moving each left next to **QtyOrdered** label and text box respectively as shown in figure 9.24
- Change the name for **QtyOrdered** Label to **Quantity** as shown in figure 9.25. Do not change the text box name in the **Detail** pane
- Click anywhere in the empty space to deselect the highlighted **Quantity** label
- Press the **Shift** key and then click each label in **Page Header** to select it
- Click the **Italic** button $\boxed{I}$ to make it upright. Click the **Center** button $\boxed{\equiv}$ to align it in the centre as shown in figure 9.25
- Click anywhere in the empty space to deselect the highlighted controls

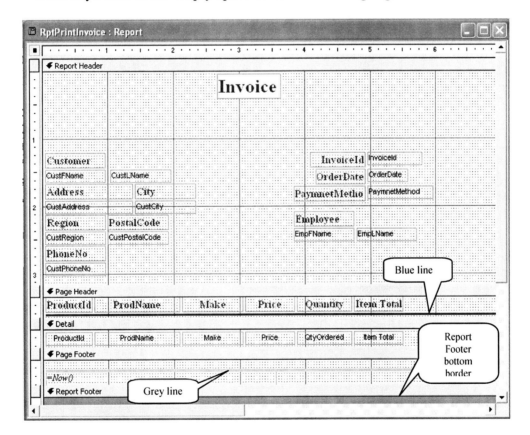

Figure 9.25

- Press the **Shift key** and then click each text box in **Detail** to select it
- Click the **Center** button to align it in the centre as shown in figure 9.25
- Click anywhere in the empty space to deselect the highlighted controls

- Double click the **Blue line** in **Page Header**. This will bring the **Properties** window for the blue line
- Select **All** tab and you will get the screen in figure 9.26

Figure 9.26

- Click in the **Width** box and then type **6"**. This will shorten the line so that it does not extend to the next page.
- Close the **Properties** window
- Double click the **Grey line** in **Page Footer**. This will bring the **Properties** window for the grey line
- Select **All** tab and then click in the **Width** box
- Type **6"** and close the window
- Scroll to the far right of **Page Footer** in figure 9.25 and you will notice the **Page Number** text box. **Delete** this text box as we do not want page numbers on our invoice
- Bring the mouse pointer to the right border of the report grid, when the pointer becomes a two headed arrow, drag it towards left so that the report can fit on a single page as shown in figure 9.27

Next we want to add a total to the end of the report

- Maximize **RptPrintInvoice** window
- Bring the mouse pointer to the bottom border of the **Report Footer** bar, when the pointer becomes a two headed arrow, drag it down to make enough space for a **Text box** as shown in figure 9.27
- Right click in the empty space in the grid and select **Toolbox**
- Click the **Text Box** button in the **Toolbox**
- Click in the right corner of the newly created space in **Report Footer**. A new **Text box** will appear in the **Report Footer** as shown in figure 9.27
- Click anywhere in the empty space to deselect the text box controls
- Click twice (not a double click) in the **Label** for the text box. Delete what is there and then type **Total:**
- Click twice in the text box (not a double click). Type **=sum([Item Total])** and then press Enter
- Right click the text box and select **Properties**

- On the **All** tab, in the **Name** box type **OrderTotal**
- Click in the **Format** box. Click the down arrow and select **Currency**
- Close the **Properties** window. Your final screen in design window should look as shown in figure 9.27

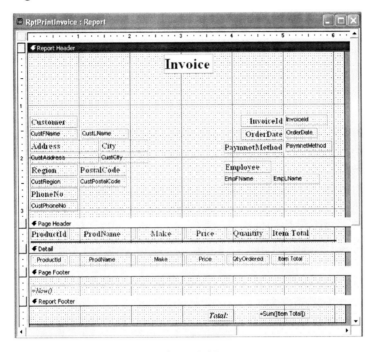

Figure 9.27

- Switch to **Report** view 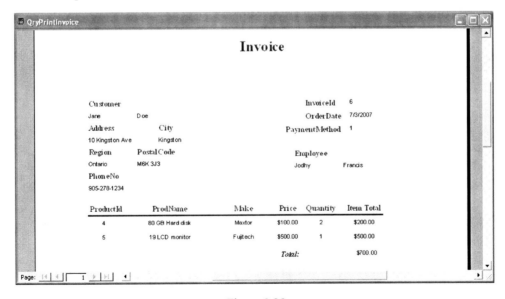 and my screen looks as shown in figure 9.28. If your screen does not look as in figure 9.28, do not worry. You will get there after a few more steps

Figure 9.28

- Close the report and save changes to the design of the report

Next we want a company logo on the invoice. A company logo appears once at the start of an invoice. Therefore, we will place the company logo in the Report header. Let us design a logo for ABC Computers

- Open Microsoft **Paint** (Start, All Programs, Accessories, Paint)
- Click the Text tab (**A**) in Microsoft Paint and then click in the top left corner in the white box. This will bring a dotted box
- Right click in the dotted box and select **Text Toolbar**. This will bring the Text Toolbar
- Select a font size of 14 and click **Bold**. Close the **Text Toolbar**
- Drag the right handle of the dotted box towards right so that the next text fit on the first line in the box
- Click back in the dotted box and type **ABC Computers**
- Click the Text tab (**A**) again and then click under ABC Computers. This will bring another dotted box
- Right click in the dotted box and select **Text Toolbar**. This will bring the Text Toolbar
- Select a font size of 10 and click **Bold** to deselect bold. Close the **Text Toolbar**
- Drag the right handle of the dotted box towards right until there is enough space to fit in the address (may be up to the right border of the white box).
- Type the following in the dotted box as shown in figure 9.29
  10 Victoria Street. Press Enter, this will take you to the next line. Type **Richmond, Ontario, M1K 3G6**. Press Enter, this will take you to the next line and then type **Phone: 905-234-1234**
- (In case the size of the white box is not the same as shown in figure 9.29 then make it to the same size) Bring the mouse pointer to the right bottom corner of the white box where it becomes a two headed arrow, then make the size of the white box to a size shown in figure 9.29

Figure 9.29

191

- Save the file as **Logo.bmp** to your **Desktop**
- Close Microsoft **Paint**
- Open **RptPrintInvoice** in **Design** view
- Right click in an empty space in **Report Header** and select **Toolbox**
- Click on the **Image** tab as shown in figure 9.30

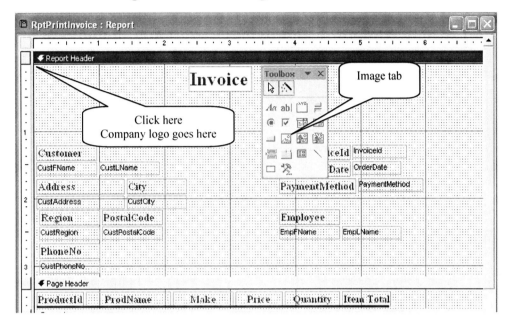

Figure 9.30

- Click in the top left corner of the **Report Header** and you will get a screen as shown in figure 9.31

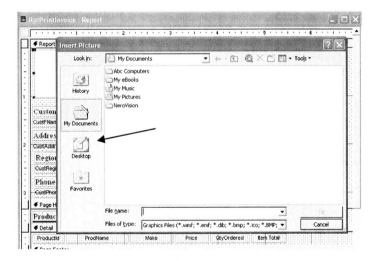

Figure 9.31

- Click **Desktop** as the company logo is saved to our desktop
- Click **Logo.bmp** from the Desktop and then click **OK**. You will get a screen as shown in figure 9.32(a)

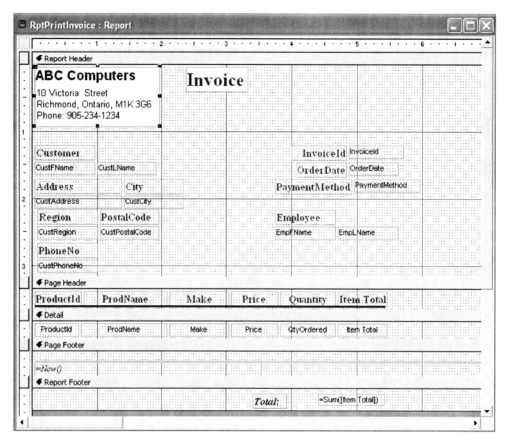

Figure 9.32 (a)

- Switch to **Report** view and you will get a screen as shown in figure 9.32 (b)

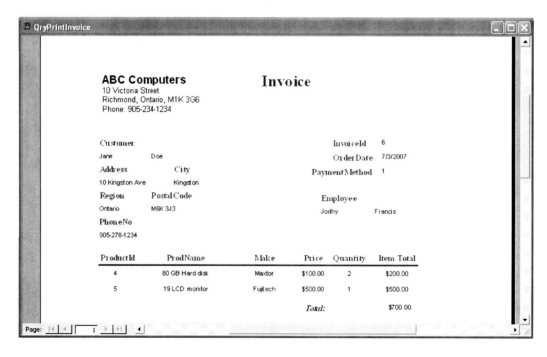

Figure 9.32(b)

- Close the report and save changes to the design of the report

When we take an order from a customer in FrmOrder, we want to print an invoice within FrmOrder. To print an invoice in FrmOrder, we need a command button.

Let us create a command button within FrmOrder that can print an invoice

- In the database window, select **Forms**
- Click **FrmOrder** and then click **Design** to open it in Design View
- Maximize the **FrmOrder** window
- Right click anywhere in the empty space and select **Toolbox**
- Click the **Command button** in the **Toolbox** to select it
- Click in the middle of the empty space under **Order Detail** subform as shown in figure 9.33. The will start the **Command button** wizard

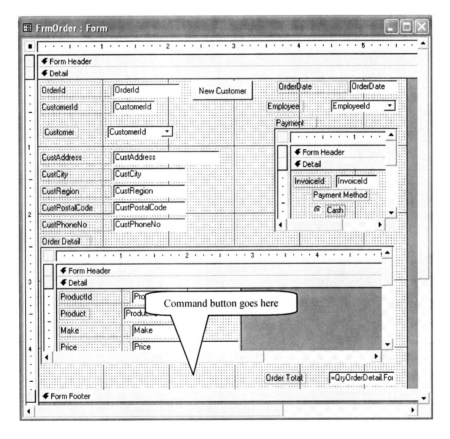

Figure 9.33

- In **Categories** select **Report Operations**
- In **Actions** select **Preview Report**. We are interested in seeing the report at this stage as we do not have a printer connected to the computer. In case we were interested in printing the report, we would select **Print Report**
- Click **Next**. The next screen comes up with a question "**What report would you like the command button to preview?**"

- Select **RptPrintInvoice**
- Click **Next**. The next screen comes up with a question "**Do you want text or a picture on the button?**
- Select **Text: Preview Report**. Click **Next**
- The next screen comes up with a question "**What do you want to name the button?**"
- Type **PrintInvoice**. Click **Finish**. You will see the screen in figure 9.34

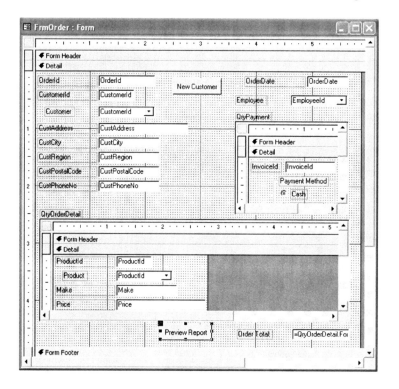

Figure 9.34

The new Command button is named as **Preview Report**. We want to change this name to **Print Invoice.**

- Right Click **Preview Report** and select **Properties**.
- Click **All** tab and you will see the screen in figure 9.35

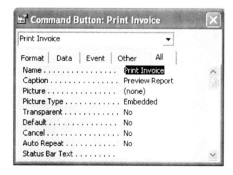

Figure 9.35

- Click in the **Caption** box. Delete the name **Preview Report**.
- Type **Print Invoice** and close the window
- Switch to **Datasheet** view and I got a screen as shown in figure 9.36

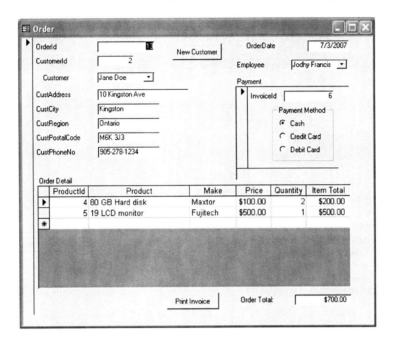

Figure 9.36

Now when a customer places an order, you enter all the required details for an order into the database. Once the order is entered, you click the Print Invoice button so that an invoice based on the current order is printed. Currently the Print Invoice button would not perform this function. To achieve this functionality, let us do the following.

- Close **FrmOrder** and save changes to the design of the form
- In database window, select **Queries**
- Select **QryPrintInvoice** and then click **Design** to open it in Design View
- Set the **Criteria** for the Field: **OrderId** to

[Forms]![FrmOrder]![OrderId]

as shown in figure 9.37. This makes the report printed for the current order

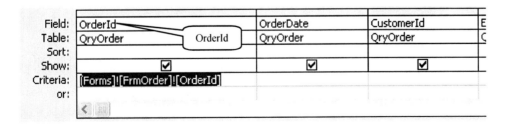

Figure 9.37

- Close the query and save changes to the design of the query
- In the database window, select **Forms**
- Double click **FrmOrder**
- Enter a new order and then click the **Print Invoice** button. An invoice for the current order is generated. My invoice looked as shown in figure 9.38

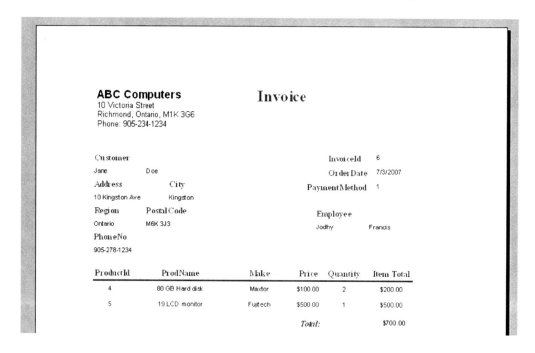

ABC Computers
10 Victoria Street
Richmond, Ontario, M1K 3G6
Phone: 905-234-1234

Invoice

Customer		InvoiceId	6
Jane	Doe	Order Date	7/3/2007
Address	City	PaymentMethod	1
10 Kingston Ave	Kingston		
Region	Postal Code	Employee	
Ontario	M6K 3J3	Jodhy	Francis
PhoneNo			
905-278-1234			

ProductId	ProdName	Make	Price	Quantity	Item Total
4	80 GB Hard disk	Maxtor	$100.00	2	$200.00
5	19 LCD monitor	Fujitech	$500.00	1	$500.00
			Total:		$700.00

Figure 9.38

This invoice in its current form gives you a rough idea on how to design an invoice. You may want to create a fancy invoice that looks much better than this. This is left as an exercise for the reader.

Creating Today's Sale Report

At the end of the day the boss wants a report that shows how much sale was done for that day. To create such a report, we need to create a query that collects the required data and then create a report based on that query. We need a query that can combine the two queries QryOrder and QryOrderDetail. As the result of each query is a table, we can join the two resulting tables from queries QryOrder and QryOrderDetail by OrderId. Then we add all the required fields from the two tables to the QBE grid.
Let us create such a query as following

- In the database window, select **Queries**
- Click **New** and you will get a window as shown in figure 9.39
- Double click **Design View**. This will bring a **Show Table** window as shown in figure 9.40
- In **Show Table** window, click on **Queries** tab

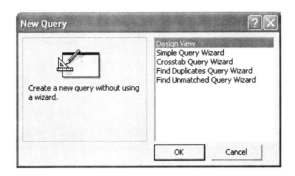

Figure 9.39

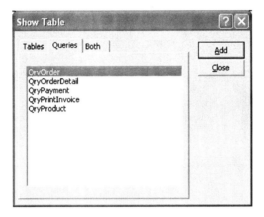

Figure 9.40

- Add **QryOrder** and **QryOrderDetail** queries to the QBE grid and then close the show table window. You will get a screen as shown in figure 9.41

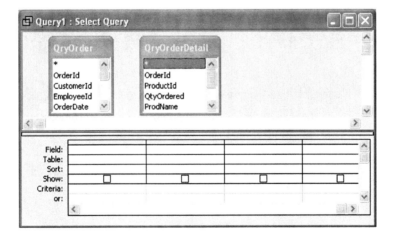

Figure 9.41

- Drag **OrderId** from table **QryOrder** to **OrderId** in **QryOrderDetail**. This will make the two tables joined by **OrderId**
- From table **QryOrder** add OrderDate to the QBE grid by double clicking the field

- From table **QryOrderDetail** add OrderId, ProductId, ProdName, Make, Price and QtyOrdered to the QBE grid by double clicking each field
- Set the **Criteria** for the field **OrderDate** to **Date()** as shown in figure 9.42. This will make the query show all the orders for today's date. If there is no order for today's date, then it will show an error

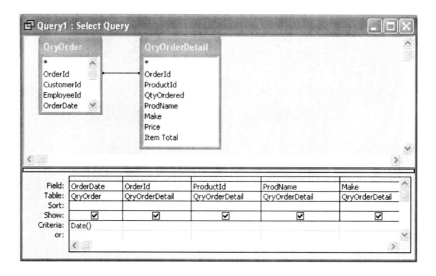

Figure 9.42

- Close the query window and you will get a screen as shown in figure 9.43

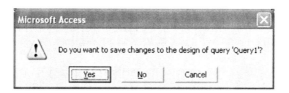

Figure 9.43

- Click **Yes**. This will bring the **Save As** window as shown in figure 9.44

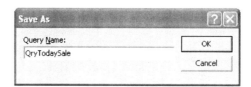

Figure 9.44

- Type **QryTodaySale** and click **Ok**. This will save the query

Next we will create a report named **RptTodaySale**. This report will be based on the information gathered in **QryTodaySale**.

- In the database window select **Reports** and then click the **New** button
- Click **Report Wizard** and then Click **Ok**. This will start the report wizard
- In the **Tables/Queries** combo box, click the down arrow and select **Query: QryTodaySale** as shown in figure 9.45

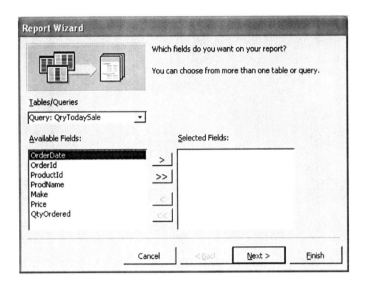

Figure 9.45

- Click the Right double arrow to move all the query fields into the **Selected Fields**
- Click **Next** and you will get a screen as shown in figure 9.46. You can select any **viewing method** from the available options. We want to view our records by **OrderDate** and it is already selected

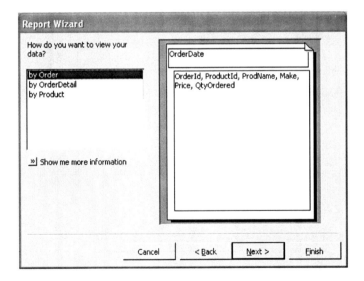

Figure 9.46

- Click **Next** and you will see a screen as shown in figure 9.47. We want to **group** our records according to **OrderId**

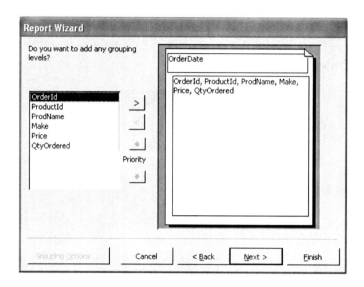

Figure 9.47

- Double click **OrderId** and a **grouping** according to OrderId is added as shown in figure 9.48

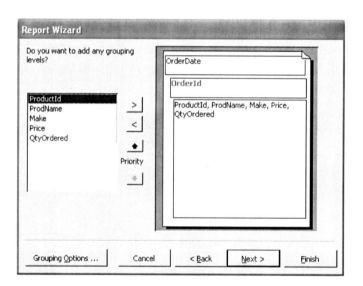

Figure 9.48

- Click **Next** and you will get a screen as shown in figure 9.49

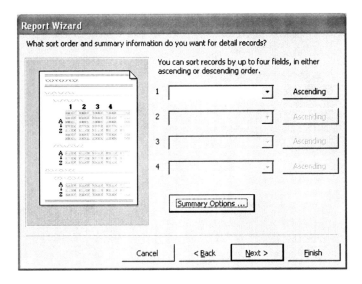

Figure 9.49

- We are not interested in any sort order. Click **Next** and you will get a screen as shown in figure 9.50

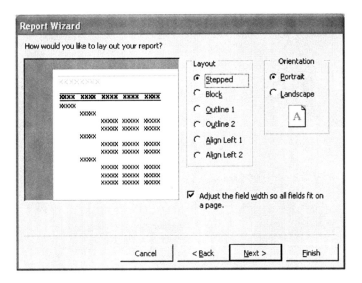

Figure 9.50

- The default **lay out** options (Stepped and Portrait) are fine. Click **Next** and you will get a screen as shown in figure 9.51

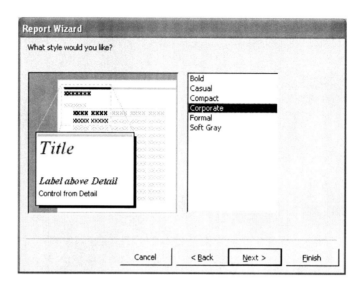

Figure 9.51

- The default **style** (Corporate) is fine. Click **Next** and you will get a screen as shown in figure 9.52

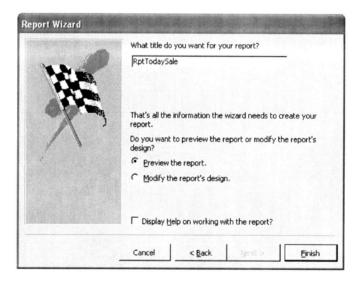

Figure 9.52

- Give the report a title of **RptTodaySale**. Leave the **Preview the report** option selected
- Click **Finish** and I got a screen as shown in figure 9.53

RptTodaySale

OrderDate OrderId		ProductId ProdName	Make
7/3/2007			
	13		
		5 19 LCD monitor	Fujitech
		4 80 GB Hard disk	Maxtor
	14		
		5 19 LCD monitor	Fujitech
		4 80 GB Hard disk	Maxtor

Figure 9.53

As you can see, the labels and its text boxes are out of place. At the end of the report, we also want a total for all the sales that was done for today. We will make the changes to the design of the report so that every thing looks nice on the report. If you have not entered any orders today, you will not see anything on the report. To see any data in this report, first you should enter a few orders into the database and then run this report.

- Open **RptTodaySale** in **Design** view and you will see a screen as shown in figure 9.54

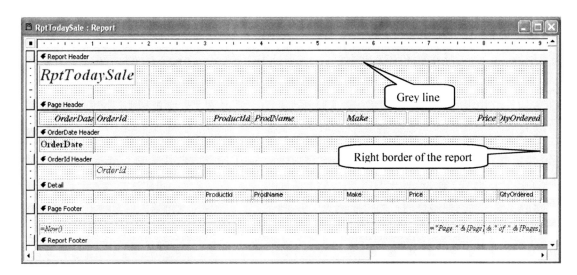

Figure 9.54

- Click on **OrderId** label in **Page Header**. Drag the right hand border towards left so that the text fit within the box
- Click on **Centre** button [icons] to align the text in the centre
- Click on **OrderId** Text box in **OrderId Header**. Drag the right hand border towards left so that the text fit within the box
- Click on **Centre** button to align the text in the centre

- Press the **Shift** key and then click **ProductId, ProdName, Make, Price** and **QtyOrdered** labels in **Page Header** to select it. Move all the selected items towards left next to **OrderId** as shown in figure 9.55
- Click anywhere in the empty space to deselect the previously selected items
- Click the **ProductId** label and then drag the right hand border towards left so that the text fit in the box
- Click anywhere in the empty space to deselect the previously selected item
- Press the **Shift** key and then click **ProdName, Make, Price** and **QtyOrdered** labels in **Page Header** to select it. Move all the selected items towards left next to **ProductId**
- Click anywhere in the empty space to deselect the previously selected items
- Click the **Price** label and then drag the right hand border towards left so that the text fit in the box
- Move the **QtyOrdered** label towards left so that it is next to **Price** Label
- Change the label for **QtyOrdered** in **Page Header** to **Quantity** and then resize it so that the text can fit in the box as shown in figure 9.56
- Resize **ProductId, ProdName, Make, Price** and **QtyOrdered** text boxes in **Detail** to match to their respective label sizes in **Page Header**
- Move all the items in **Detail** towards left so that they are under their respective labels in **Page Header** as shown in figure 9.56
- Do not change the name for **QtyOrdered** text box in **Detail** and leave it the way it is shown in figure 9.56

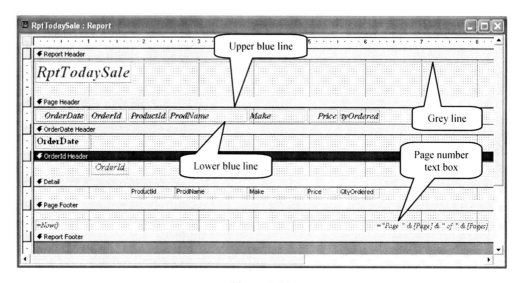

Figure 9.55

- Click the **Page number** text box in **Page Footer**. Drag the right hand border towards left so that the text fits within the box
- Next move the text box towards left so that it aligned nicely with in the page as shown in figure 9.56
- Double click the **Grey line** in **Report Header**. This will bring the **Properties** window for the line.
- In the **Width** box, type **6"** and close the window

- Bring the mouse pointer to the top border of **OrderDate Header**. When it becomes a two headed arrow, drag the border downward so that you can see the lower blue line within the **Page Header**
- Double click the **Lower Blue line**. This will bring the **Properties** window for the line
- In the **Width** box, type **6"** and close the window
- Bring the mouse pointer to the top border of **OrderDate Header**. When it becomes a two headed arrow, drag the border upward to where it was
- Double click the **Upper Blue line** in **Page Header**. This will bring the **Properties** window for the line
- In the **Width** box, type **6"** and close the window
- Bring the mouse pointer to the right border of the **Report grid**. You may have to scroll towards right. When the mouse pointer changes to a two headed arrow, drag the border towards left so that it aligns with the rest of the page as shown in figure 9.56
- Click on **ProductId** text box in **Detail**. Click on **Centre** to align the text in the centre
- Click the label for **ProdName** in **Page Header** and then click on **Centre** to align it in the centre
- Change the label for **ProdName** in **Page Header** to **Product**
- Click the text box for **ProdName** in **Detail** and align it in the **Centre**
- Click the label for **Price** in **Page Header** and align it left as shown in figure 9.56

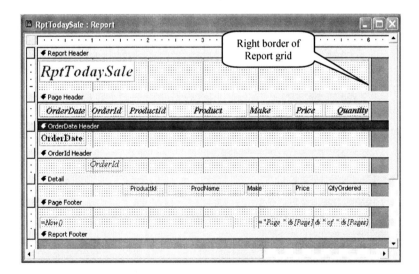

Figure 9.56

Next we want to add a total to the end of the report for that day

- Bring the mouse pointer to the bottom border of the **Report Footer** bar and when the pointer becomes a two headed arrow, drag it down to make enough space for a Text box
- Right click in the empty space in the grid and select **Toolbox**

- Click the **Text Box** button in the **Toolbox**
- Click in the right corner of the newly created space in **Report Footer**. A new text box appears in the form footer as shown in figure 9.57
- Click anywhere in the empty space to deselect the text box controls
- Click twice (not a double click) inside the **Label** and type **Total:**
- Click twice inside the **Text box** (not a double click) and type **=sum([Price]*[QtyOrdered])** and then press Enter
- Right click the **Text box** and click **Properties**
- Click the **All** tab, in the **Name** box type **TodayTotal**
- Click in the **Format** box. Click the down arrow and select **Currency**
- Close the **Properties** window. Your screen in design view should look as shown in figure 9.57

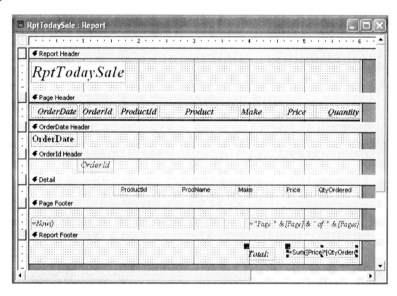

Figure 9.57

- Switch to **Report** view and my screen looks as shown in figure 9.58

RptTodaySale

OrderDate	OrderId	ProductId	Product	Make	Price	Quantity
7/3/2007						
	13					
		5	19 LCD monitor	Fujitech	$500.00	2
		4	80 GB Hard disk	Maxtor	$100.00	2
	14					
		5	19 LCD monitor	Fujitech	$500.00	3
		4	80 GB Hard disk	Maxtor	$100.00	1
			Total:		$2,800.00	

Figure 9.58

- Close the report and save changes to the design of the report

Creating a Date Range Report

Sometime your boss wants a report that spans from one date to another. Consider he asks you for last month's sale report so that he can find out who is the most valuable customer for that month. At the end of year, he may ask you for a full year report to find the most valuable customer for that year. To create such a report, we can use a date range report. In a date range report, you enter a beginning date and ending date for the report.

We can amend the existing QryTodaySale query to suite our needs. Let us change the existing query to a parameter query for the new report.

- In the database window, select **Queries**
- Right click **QryTodaySale** and select **Save As**
- Type **QryDateRange** as shown in figure 9.59. Click **Ok**

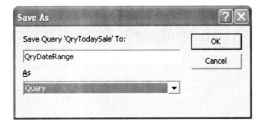

Figure 9.59

- Click **QryDateRange** and then click **Design**
- Maximize the window
- In the QBE grid as shown in figure 9.60, drag the right border for **OrderDate** field towards right so that you can see all the typing in the **Criteria**
- In the **Criteria** for **OrderDate** field, delete **Date()**. Type

Between [Beginning date mm/dd/yyyy] And [Ending date mm/dd/yyyy]

as shown in figure 9.60

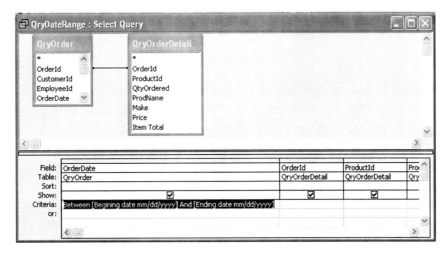

Figure 9.60

- Close the window and save changes to the design of the query
- In the database window, select **Reports**
- Right click **RptTodaySale** and select **Save As**
- Type **RptDateRange** as shown in figure 9.61. Click **Ok**

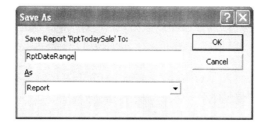

Figure 9.61

- Open **RptDateRange** in **Design** View as shown in figure 9.62

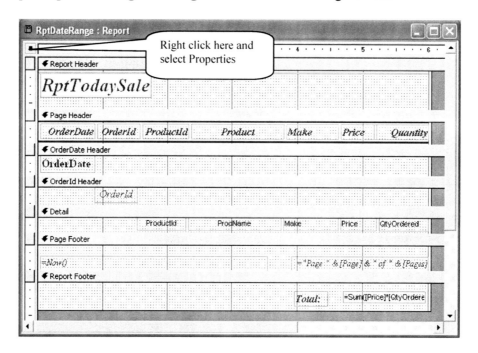

Figure 9.62

- Right click inside the box with a black dot as shown in figure 9.62
- Select **Properties**. This will bring the properties window for the report
- Select the **All** tab, click in **Record Source** box
- Click the down arrow and select **QryDateRange**
- Click in **Caption** box. Delete **RptTodaySale** and type **RptDateRange**
- Close the **Properties** window
- In **Report Header**, click in **RptTodaySale** box as shown in figure 9.62
- Delete **RptTodaySale**. Type **RptDateRange**
- Switch to **Report** view and you will get a screen as shown in figure 9.63

Figure 9.63

- Type a beginning date in **mm/dd/yyyy** format. I typed **07/01/2007**
- Click **Ok**. You will get a screen as shown in figure 9.64

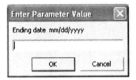

Figure 9.64

- Type an ending date in **mm/dd/yyyy** format. I typed **07/30/2007**
- Click **Ok**. I got a screen as shown in figure 9.65

RptDateRange

OrderDate	OrderId	ProductId	Product	Make	Price	Quantity
7/3/2007						
	13					
		5	19 LCD monitor	Fujitech	$500.00	2
		4	80 GB Hard disk	Maxtor	$100.00	2
	14					
		5	19 LCD monitor	Fujitech	$500.00	3
		4	80 GB Hard disk	Maxtor	$100.00	1
7/5/2007						
	16					
		6	6 PPM Printer	Lexmark	$250.00	1
		5	19 LCD monitor	Fujitech	$500.00	1
		7	1 GB RAM	Samsung	$300.00	1
	17					
		8	17 Monitor	Samsung	$300.00	1
		9	DVD Burner	Panasonic	$200.00	1
				Total:	$4,350.00	

Figure 9.65

- Close the window and save changes to the design of the report

Make sure that you have orders in the database for the date range that you are entering. If you enter a date range that does not have any orders, it will show an error.

Creating an Inventory Report

At the end of the week, the boss wants to know how much inventory is in stock. To produce such a report, we need to create a query that is based on the Product table. Let us start creating such a query

- In the database window, select **Queries** and click **New**. This will bring a window as shown in figure 9.66

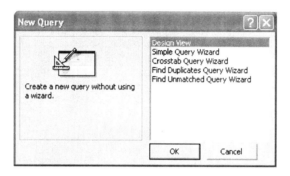

Figure 9.66

- Select **Design View** and click **Ok**. A **Show table** window will appear on the top of Select Query window as shown in figure 9.67

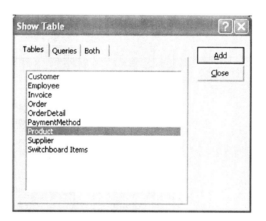

Figure 9.67

- Select **Product** table and then click **Add**
- Click **Close**. The **Product** table will appear in the **Select Query** window
- In the **Product** table, double click the fields ProductId, ProdName, Make and QtyInStock to add it to the query grid. You will get a query grid as shown in figure 9.68

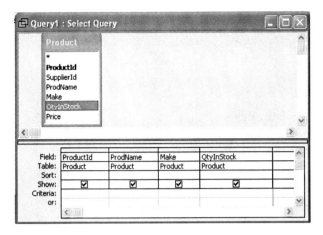

Figure 9.68

- Click in the **Criteria** for **QtyInStock** and type **> 0**

We are selecting a Criteria greater then zero for QtyInStock because we want to know how much supplies are in stock.

- **Close** the query. You will get a screen as shown in figure 9.69

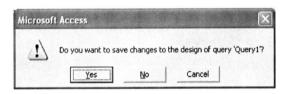

Figure 9.69

- Click **Yes** and a screen as shown in figure 9.70 will appear

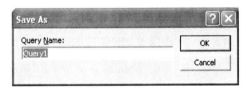

Figure 9.70

- Type **QryInventoryInStock** in the **Save As** box
- Click **Ok** and the screen will disappear
- In **Queries** window, double click **QryInventoryInStock** and I got a screen as shown in figure 9.71

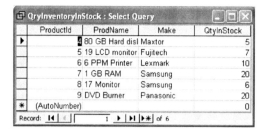

Figure 9.71

- Close this window
- In the database window, select **Reports** and click **New**
- Select **Report Wizard**
- Select **QryInventoryInStock** in the bottom list box and click **Ok**

This will bring the screen in figure 9.72. As you can see in the figure, you are given the choice of what fields to add to the report.

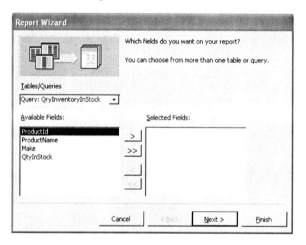

Figure 9.72

- Add all the fields to the **Selected Fields** list by clicking the right double arrow
- Click **Next**. The second wizard step appears as shown in figure 9.73

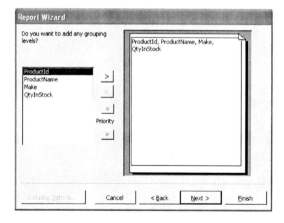

Figure 9.73

- We do not want any **grouping levels**. Click **Next**
- The third wizard step appears and gives you the choice of a **sort order** for your records as shown in figure 9.74.
- Click the first down arrow and select **Make**. Click **Next**.

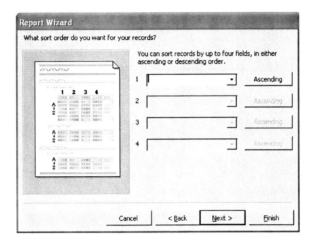

Figure 9.74

- The fourth wizard step appears and gives you the choice of a **lay out** for your report as shown in figure 9.75. The default lay out (Tabular and Portrait) is fine for this report. Click **Next**

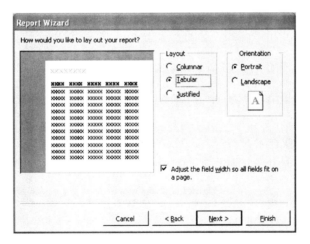

Figure 9.75

- The fifth wizard step appears as shown in figure 9.76. This step gives you the choice of six **styles** for your report. Leave the default (Corporate) style. Click **Next**

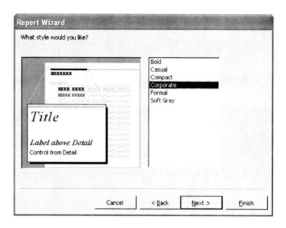

Figure 9.76

- The last wizard step appears as shown in figure 9.77. Give the report a name of **RptInventoryInStock**

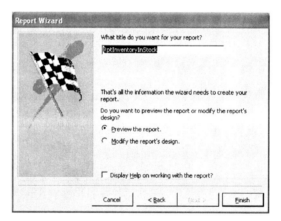

Figure 9.77

- Click **Finish**. This will create a report and mine looks as shown in figure 9.78

RptInventoryInStock

Make	ProductId	ProdName	QtyInStock
Fujitech	5	19 LCD monitor	7
Lexmark	6	6 PPM Printer	10
Maxtor	4	80 GB Hard disk	5
Panasonic	9	DVD Burner	20
Samsung	8	17 Monitor	6
Samsung	7	1 GB RAM	20

Figure 9.78

The layout of this report is not right. Let us change its layout.

- Switch to **Design** view and you will get a screen as shown in figure 9.79

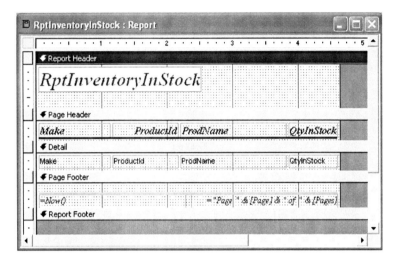

Figure 9.79

- Make it look as shown in figure 9.80. This is an exercise for the reader. As a hint, the label for **ProdName** in **Page Header** has been changed to **Product**

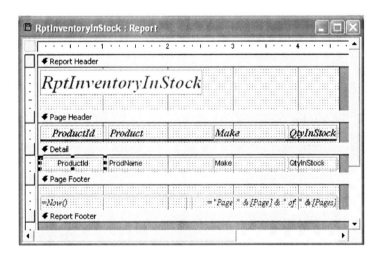

Figure 9.80

- Switch to **Report** View and I got a screen as shown in figure 9.81

RptInventoryInStock

ProductId	Product	Make	QtyInStock
5	19 LCD monitor	Fujitech	7
6	6 PPM Printer	Lexmark	10
4	80 GB Hard disk	Maxtor	5
9	DVD Burner	Panasonic	20
8	17 Monitor	Samsung	6
7	1 GB RAM	Samsung	20

Figure 9.81

- Close the report and save changes to the design of the report

Chapter 10

The Switchboard

The database that we created is a collection of interrelated database objects that can be used by someone who knows Access. For someone who does not know Access, it may not be so easy. In this chapter we will tie the database objects together into an application that allows the end user to focus on the data instead of how to use Access. The switchboard is a primary component of any Access application that serves as a central point for opening objects in your database.

The switchboard is a form that contains command buttons. The command buttons run macros that perform tasks such as opening forms and reports. The user does not have to search for any form or report through the whole database because all the objects are located at one central point in the switchboard.

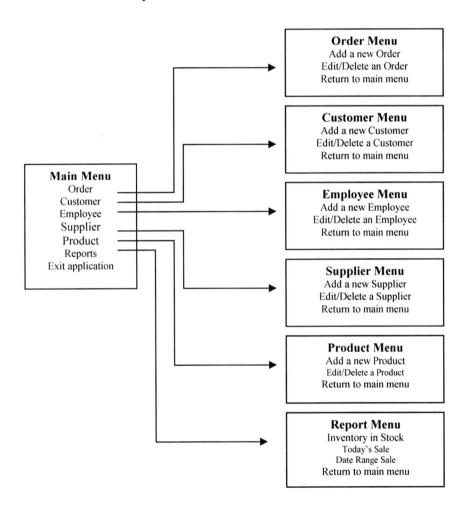

Figure 10.1

Planning a Switchboard

The first thing that we are going to do is to decide on how the user interface should look. This involves a careful design of the menu structure. We have chosen the menu structure shown in figure 10.1

As you can see, there is a hierarchy in the menu structure. This structure suits best our needs. We will build our switchboard according to this structure.

Creating a Switchboard

- Click on **Tools, Database Utilities, Switchboard Manager** and you will get a screen as shown in figure 10.2

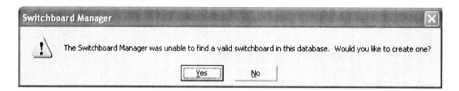

Figure 10.2

- Click **Yes**. The **Switchboard Manager** window opens as shown in figure 10.3

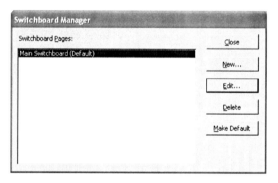

Figure 10.3

- Click **New** and you will see a screen as shown in figure 10.4

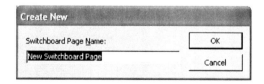

Figure 10.4

- Type **Order Menu** and click **Ok**. This will create the first submenu as shown in figure 10.5

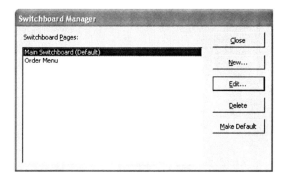

Figure 10.5

- Click **New** again. Type **Customer Menu** and click **Ok**
- Click **New**. Type **Employee Menu** and click **Ok**
- Click **New**. Type **Supplier Menu** and click **Ok**
- Click **New**. Type **Product Menu** and click **Ok**
- Click **New**. Type **Report Menu** and click **Ok**
- Click **New**. Type **Exit Application** and click **Ok**

After doing all this, you will get a screen as shown in figure 10.6.

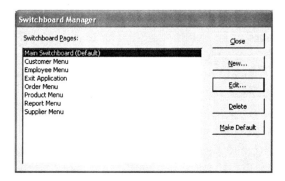

Figure 10.6

As you can see, Access placed all the menu items in alphabetic order. Next we want each main menu item to have a submenu as shown in figure 10.1. To do that, we will edit each menu item in the Switchboard Manager.

- In the **Switchboard Manager** in figure 10.6, click on **Customer Menu** and then click on **Edit**. The **Edit Switchboard Page** window will appear as shown in figure 10.7

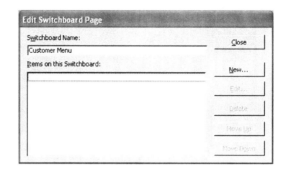

Figure 10.7

- Click **New** and the **Edit Switchboard Item** window will appear as shown in figure 10.8

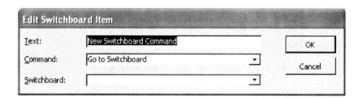

Figure 10.8

In this window, in the **Text:** you have to specify the text that appears next to the menu button. In the **Command:** you specify the action the button will perform. The **Switchboard:** depends on what you choose in Command window and then select the right option for that. Let us take these actions for each menu

- In the **Text:** Type **Add a new Customer**
- In the **Command:** Click the down arrow and select **Open Form in Add Mode**
- In the **Form:** Click the down arrow and select **FrmCustomer**. You will get a screen as shown in figure 10.9

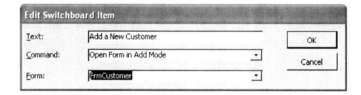

Figure 10.9

- Click **Ok** and this will bring you back to **Edit Switchboard Page** window as shown in figure 10.10

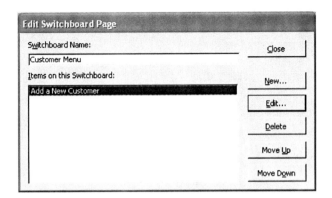

Figure 10.10

- Click **New** again and the **Edit Switchboard Item** window will appear
- In the **Text:** Type **Edit/Delete a Customer**
- In the **Command:** Click the down arrow and select **Open Form in Edit Mode**
- In the **Form:** Click the down arrow and select **FrmCustomer**. You will see a screen as shown in figure 10.11

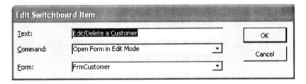

Figure 10.11

- Click **OK**. You will see a Screen as shown in figure 10.12

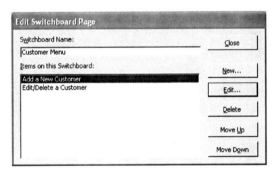

Figure 10.12

- Click **New** again and the **Edit Switchboard Item** window will appear
- In the **Text:** Type **Return to Main Menu**
- In the **Command:** Click the down arrow and select **Go to Switchboard**
- In the **Switchboard:** Click the down arrow and select **Main Switchboard** as shown in figure 10.13

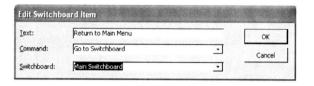

Figure 10.13

- Click **OK**. You will see a screen as shown in figure 10.14

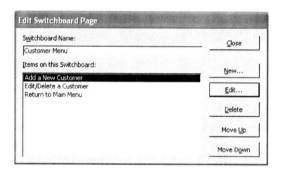

Figure 10.14

- Click **Close** and you will be back in **Switchboard Manager** screen as shown in figure 10.15

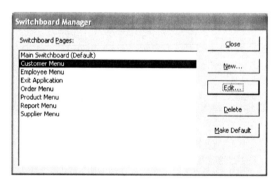

Figure 10.15

We will repeat the same steps for each menu item

- In the **Switchboard Manager**, click on **Employee Menu** and then click on **Edit**. The **Edit Switchboard Page** window will appear
- Click **New** in the **Edit Switchboard Page** window. This will bring **Edit Switchboard Item** window
- Type **Add a New Employee** as the **Text**. Select **Open Form in Add Mode** as the **Command**. Select **FrmEmployee** as the **Form**. Click **Ok**.
- Click **New** again in the **Edit Switchboard Page** window. This will bring **Edit Switchboard Item** window

- Type **Edit/Delete an Employee** as the **Text**. Select **Open Form in Edit Mode** as the **Command**. Select **FrmEmployee** as the **Form**. Click **Ok**.
- Click **New** again in the **Edit Switchboard Page** window. This will bring **Edit Switchboard Item** window
- Type **Return to Main Menu** as the **Text**. Select **Go to Switchboard** as the **Command**. Select **Main Switchboard** as the **Switchboard**. Click **Ok**.
- Click **Close** to return to **Switchboard Manager** window

- In the **Switchboard Manager**, click on **Order Menu** and then click on **Edit**. The **Edit Switchboard Page** window will appear
- Click **New** in the **Edit Switchboard Page** window. This will bring **Edit Switchboard Item** window
- Type **Add a New Order** as the **Text**. Select **Open Form in Add Mode** as the **Command**. Select **FrmOrder** as the **Form**. Click **Ok**
- Click **New** again in the **Edit Switchboard Page** window. This will bring **Edit Switchboard Item** window
- Type **Edit/Delete an Order** as the **Text**. Select **Open Form in Edit Mode** as the **Command**. Select **FrmOrder** as the **Form**. Click **Ok**
- Click **New** again in the **Edit Switchboard Page** window. This will bring **Edit Switchboard Item** window
- Type **Return to Main Menu** as the **Text**. Select **Go to Switchboard** as the **Command**. Select **Main Switchboard** as the **Switchboard**. Click **Ok**
- Click **Close** to return to **Switchboard Manager** window

- In the **Switchboard Manager**, click on **Product Menu** and then click on **Edit**. The **Edit Switchboard Page** window will appear
- Click **New** in the **Edit Switchboard Page** window. This will bring **Edit Switchboard Item** window
- Type **Add a New Product** as the **Text**. Select **Open Form in Add Mode** as the **Command**. Select **FrmProduct** as the **Form**. Click **Ok**
- Click **New** again in the **Edit Switchboard Page** window. This will bring **Edit Switchboard Item** window
- Type **Edit/Delete a Product** as the **Text**. Select **Open Form in Edit Mode** as the **Command**. Select **FrmProduct** as the **Form**. Click **Ok**
- Click **New** again in the **Edit Switchboard Page** window. This will bring **Edit Switchboard Item** window
- Type **Return to Main Menu** as the **Text**. Select **Go to Switchboard** as the **Command**. Select **Main Switchboard** as the **Switchboard**. Click **Ok**
- Click **Close** to return to **Switchboard Manager** window

- In the **Switchboard Manager**, click on **Report Menu** and then click on **Edit**. The **Edit Switchboard Page** window will appear
- Click **New** in the **Edit Switchboard Page** window. This will bring **Edit Switchboard Item** window

- Type **Inventory in Stock** as the **Text**. Select **Open Report** as the **Command**. Select **RptInventoryInStock** as the **Report**. Click **OK**
- Click **New** again in the **Edit Switchboard Page** window. This will bring **Edit Switchboard Item** window
- Type **Today's Sale** as the **Text**. Select **Open Report** as the **Command**. Select **RptTodaySale** as the **Report**. Click **Ok**
- Click **New** again in the **Edit Switchboard Page** window. This will bring **Edit Switchboard Item** window
- Type **Date Range Sale** as the **Text**. Select **Open Report** as the **Command**. Select **RptDateRange** as the **Report**. Click **Ok**
- Click **New** again in the **Edit Switchboard Page** window. This will bring **Edit Switchboard Item** window
- Type **Return to Main Menu** as the **Text**. Select **Go to Switchboard** as the **Command**. Select **Main Switchboard** as the **Switchboard**. Click **Ok**
- Click **Close** to return to **Switchboard Manager** window

- In the **Switchboard Manager**, click on **Supplier Menu** and then click on **Edit**. The **Edit Switchboard Page** window will appear
- Click **New** in the **Edit Switchboard Page** window. This will bring **Edit Switchboard Item** window
- Type **Add a New Supplier** as the **Text**. Select **Open Form in Add Mode** as the **Command**. Select **FrmSupplier** as the **Form**. Click **Ok**
- Click **New** again in the **Edit Switchboard Page** window. This will bring **Edit Switchboard Item** window
- Type **Edit/Delete a Supplier** as the **Text**. Select **Open Form in Edit Mode** as the **Command**. Select **FrmSupplier** as the **Form**. Click **Ok**
- Click **New** again in the **Edit Switchboard Page** window. This will bring **Edit Switchboard Item** window
- Type **Return to Main Menu** as the **Text**. Select **Go to Switchboard** as the **Command**. Select **Main Switchboard** as the **Switchboard**. Click **Ok**
- Click **Close** to return to **Switchboard Manager** window

For every item in the Main Menu, we created a submenu. If you want to use the switchboard in its exiting form, it will not work as we have not created the Main Menu yet. We still have to do a little bit of more work to make the switchboard functional.

- Click **Close** in **Switchboard Manager** window
- In the **Forms** window, you will notice a new **Switchboard** form. Double click **Switchboard** form. You will see the screen shown in figure 10.16

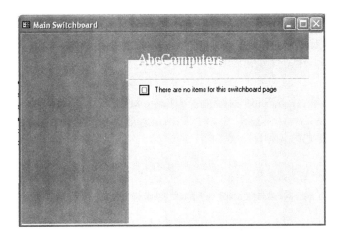

Figure 10.16

The switchboard is empty and says that "There are no items for this switchboard page". This shows that we have not created the main menu in the switchboard. All the work that we did before was related to the submenus in the Main Switchboard

- Close the **Main Switchboard** form
- Click **Tools, Database Utilities, Switchboard Manager**
- Select **Main Switchboard (Default)** and then click **Edit**
- Click **New** in the **Edit Switchboard Page** window and you will see a screen as shown in figure 10.17

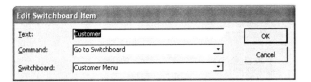

Figure 10.17

- Type **Customer** as the **Text**. Select **Go to Switchboard** as the **Command**. Select **Customer Menu** as the **Switchboard**. Click **Ok**

- Click **New** again in the **Edit Switchboard Page** window. Type **Employee** as the **Text**. Select **Go to Switchboard** as the **Command**. Select **Employee Menu** as the **Switchboard**. Click **Ok**

- Click **New** in the **Edit Switchboard Page** window. Type **Order** as the **Text**. Select **Go to Switchboard** as the **Command**. Select **Order Menu** as the **Switchboard**. Click **Ok**.

- Click **New** in the **Edit Switchboard Page** window. Type **Product** as the **Text**. Select **Go to Switchboard** as the **Command**. Select **Product Menu** as the **Switchboard**. Click **Ok**

- Click **New** in the **Edit Switchboard Page** window. Type **Report** as the **Text**. Select **Go to Switchboard** as the **Command**. Select **Report Menu** as the **Switchboard**. Click **Ok**

- Click **New** in the **Edit Switchboard Page** window. Type **Supplier** as the **Text**. Select **Go to Switchboard** as the **Command**. Select **Supplier Menu** as the **Switchboard**. Click **Ok**

- Click **New** in the **Edit Switchboard Page** window. Type **Exit Application** as the **Text**. Select **Exit Application** as the **Command**. You will get a screen as shown in figure 10.18

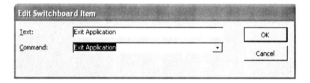

Figure 10.18

- Click **Ok**

After adding all the menu items to the Main Switchboard (Default), your Edit Switchboard Page will look as shown in figure 10.19

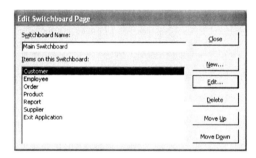

Figure 10.19

- Click **Close** to return to **Switchboard Manager** window as shown in figure 10.20

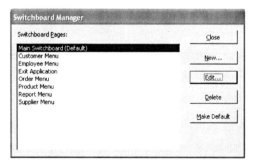

Figure 10.20

- Click **Close** in **Switchboard Manager** window to get out of it
- In the **Forms** window, double click **Switchboard**. You will get a screen as shown in figure 10.21

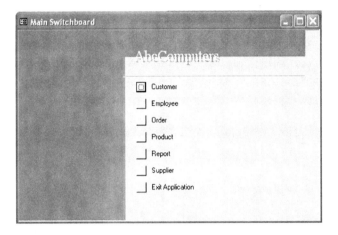

Figure 10.21

Click on each button and navigate through the menus. Once every button is working properly, your Switchboard is complete.

Setting up Startup Options

- Click on **Tools** and then select **Startup**. You will see the screen in figure 10.22

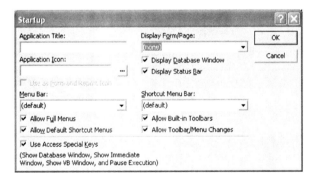

Figure 10.22

We want the switchboard to load automatically when the application is started. To do this, do the following

- In the **Display Form/Page:** click the down arrow, select **Switchboard**. This will load the Switchboard when you start the application

We also want the name ABC Computers to appear in the Title Bar at the top of Access screen. To do this, do the following

- While still in the **Startup** window, in the **Application Title** box, type **ABC Computers**
- Click **Ok**
- Close the application
- Open **ABC Computers** database

When you open ABC Computers database, the Switchboard will open as shown in figure 10.23. From here you can select any function you want within the application. You would also notice that the application is displaying a title of ABC Computers. This shows that the changes that we made to the startup options works fine.

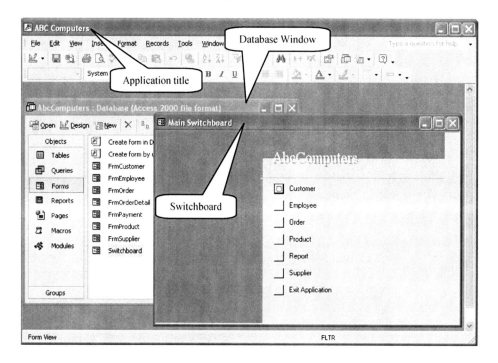

Figure 10.23

Finishing Touches

Here we will address the system requirement issue briefly. During "Identifying System Requirements" phase in chapter 4, you asked Mr. Brown the following question.

You: Is any data confidential?
Owner: I would like to have the database password protected.

We can provide protection to our database by adding a password. For more intensive security, you should use user level security. As the owner is just asking for password protection, we will only add password security.

- Close the **Main Switchboard** in 10.23
- Close the **Database window** in 10.23
- Click **File**, Click **Open**. I got a screen as shown in figure 10.24

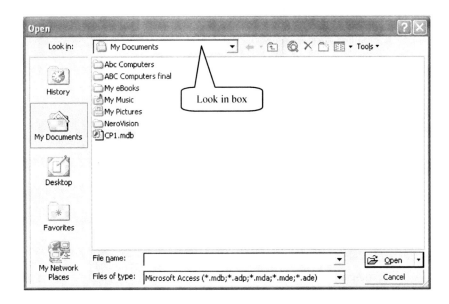

Figure 10.24

- Click the arrow to the right of the **Look In** box. Select **Local Disk (C:)**
- Double Click **ABC Computers** folder as this is the location of our database
- Click **ABC Computers.mdb**
- Click the arrow to the right of the **Open** button as shown in figure 10.25
- Click **Open Exclusive** and the database will be opened in exclusive mode

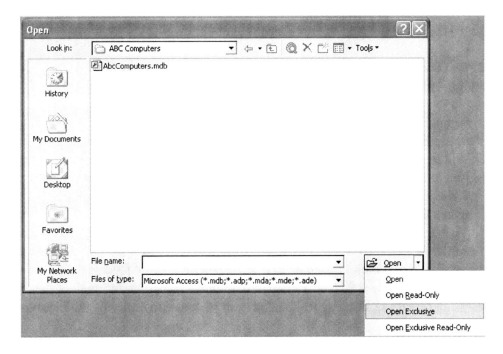

Figure 10.25

- Click **Tools**, point to **Security** and then click **Set Database Password**. You will get a screen as shown in figure 10.26

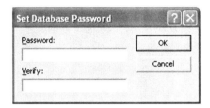

Figure 10.26

- In the **Password** box type your password (I used the word **password**)
- In the **Verify** box confirm your password (I typed **password**)
- Click **Ok.** The password is now set
- Close the database
- Open **ABC Computers** database. You will get a screen asking for a password as shown in figure 10.27

Figure 10.27

- Enter the password and the database will open

The other two questions that you asked Mr. Brown during "Identifying System Requirements" phase were:

You: How long do you want to keep the data?
Owner: I would like to keep data on customers for 3 years so that we know our customer's interests and we can mail them flyers on special offers. We also need this data for accounting purposes.
You: What kind of protection from failure do you want for your database?
Owner: I need a backup of the database during non business hours.

You can use the data in the database as long as there is no corruption of the database or any hardware failure. The maximum size of a Microsoft Access database can not exceed 2 gigabytes minus the space needed for system objects. To safeguard against database corruption or hardware failure, a good backup and restore capability of the database is necessary.

To get a good backup, you need a combination of software and hardware. Picking up the right hardware and software depend on your budget and your needs. You can also backup your database to your local hard disk without buying any new hardware. The bad thing about this option is that when the hard disk fails, your backup is gone. A better option would be to buy a DLT tape drive or some other hardware for the backup. You attach the newly bought tape drive to your computer and then install a driver for the new device.

Next you need a good backup software that can direct the backup and manage the data. Windows comes with its own backup software. You can also buy backup software from other vendors like Veritas. They have a very good product called Backupexec. In our case, it is strongly recommended that you backup the local drive C: where the database and the Operating system files reside. In case the local drive fails, we can restore the whole drive C:. It is also recommended that you do an incremental backup during the week nights and do a full backup on the weekend. An incremental backup will only backup the files that have changed. A full backup will backup every thing that is on that drive. Open files do not get backed up during backup. Make sure that nobody is in the database when the backup is running. If you follow this advice, you will be able to restore the database in case of a disaster.

References

Modern Database Management, 6th Edition. Fred R. McFadden, Jaffrey A. Hoffer, Mary B. Prescott:
Addison-Wesley
Database Solutions: A step-by-step guide to building databases. Thomas Connolly, Carolyn Begg:
Addison-Wesley
Database Design for Mere Mortals, 2nd Edition. Michael J. Hernandez:
Addison-Wesley
Database Systems Design, Implementation, & Management, 5th Edition. Peter Rob, Carlos Coronel:
Course Technology
The Relational Database. John Carter:
Chapman & Hall
Inside Relational Databases: with examples in Access. Mark Whitehorn, Bill Marklyn
Springer

Printed in the United States
128535LV00001B/52/P

9 781435 707986